ADOBE
Photoshop®
Elements 6

CLASSROOM IN A BOOK

www.adobepress.com

Adobe

Notice to U.S. Government End Users. The Software and Documentation are "Commercial Items," as that term is defined at 48 C.F.R. §2.101, consisting of "Commercial Computer Software" and "Commercial Computer Software Documentation," as such terms are used in 48 C.F.R. §12.212 or 48 C.F.R. §227.7202, as applicable. Consistent with 48 C.F.R. §12.212 or 48 C.F.R. §§227.7202-1 through 227.7202-4, as applicable, the Commercial Computer Software and Commercial Computer Software Documentation are being licensed to U.S. Government end users (a) only as Commercial Items and (b) with only those rights as are granted to all other end users pursuant to the terms and conditions herein. Unpublished-rights reserved under the copyright laws of the United States. Adobe Systems Incorporated, 345 Park Avenue, San Jose, CA 95110-2704, USA. For U.S. Government End Users, Adobe agrees to comply with all applicable equal opportunity laws including, if appropriate, the provisions of Executive Order 11246, as amended, Section 402 of the Vietnam Era Veterans Readjustment Assistance Act of 1974 (38 USC 4212), and Section 503 of the Rehabilitation Act of 1973, as amended, and the regulations at 41 CFR Parts 60-1 through 60-60, 60-250, and 60-741. The affirmative action clause and regulations contained in the preceding sentence shall be incorporated by reference.

Adobe Press books are published by Peachpit, Berkeley, CA. To report errors, please send a note to errata@peachpit.com.

Printed in the U.S.A.

ISBN-13: 978-0-321-52465-2
ISBN-10:   0-321-52465-9

9 8 7 6 5 4 3 2 1

Lesson files . . . and so much more

The *Adobe Photoshop Elements 6.0 Classroom in a Book* CD includes the lesson files that you'll need to complete the exercises in this book, as well as other content to help you learn more about Adobe Photoshop Elements and use it with greater efficiency and ease. The diagram below represents the contents of the CD, which should help you locate the files you need.

Lessons

Each lesson has its own folder inside the Lessons folder. You will need to copy these lesson folders to your hard disk before you can begin each lesson.

Adobe Press

Find information about other Adobe Press titles, covering the full spectrum of Adobe products, in the Adobe Press folder.

Contents

Getting Started

1 A Quick Tour of Photoshop Elements

2   Basic Organizing

3   Advanced Organizing

4   Creating Projects

5 Printing, Sharing, and Exporting

6 Adjusting Color in Images

<table>
<tr><td>7</td><td>Fixing Exposure Problems</td></tr>
</table>

8 Repairing and Retouching Images

9   Working with Text

10   Combining Multiple Images

11   **Advanced Editing Techniques**

Getting Started

Adobe® Photoshop® Elements 6.0 delivers image-editing tools that balance power and versatility with ease of use. Photoshop Elements 6.0 is ideal for home users, hobbyists, business users, and professional photographers—anyone who wants to produce good-looking pictures and sophisticated graphics for the Web and for print.

If you've used earlier versions of Photoshop Elements, you'll find that this Classroom in a Book® teaches many advanced skills and describes innovative features that Adobe Systems has introduced in this version. If you're new to Adobe Photoshop Elements 6.0, you'll learn the fundamental concepts and techniques that help you master the application.

About Classroom in a Book

Adobe Photoshop Elements 6.0 Classroom in a Book is part of the official training series for Adobe graphics and publishing software developed by Adobe product experts. Each lesson in this book is made up of a series of self-paced projects that give you hands-on experience using Photoshop Elements 6.0.

The *Adobe Photoshop Elements 6.0 Classroom in a Book* includes a CD attached to the inside back cover of this book. On the CD you'll find all the image files used for the lessons in this book, along with additional learning resources.

Prerequisites

Before you begin working on the lessons in this book, make sure that you and your computer are ready.

Requirements on your computer

You'll need about 400 MB of free space on your hard disk for the lesson files and the work files you'll create. The lesson files necessary for your work in this book are on the CD attached to the inside back cover of this book.

Required skills

The lessons in the *Adobe Photoshop Elements 6.0 Classroom in a Book* assume that you have a working knowledge of your computer and its operating system. This book does not teach the most basic and generic computer skills. If you can answer yes to the following questions, then you're probably well qualified to start working on the projects in these lessons. Most users should work on the lessons in the order in which they occur in the book.

• Do you know how to use the Microsoft Windows Start button and the Windows Taskbar? Can you open menus and submenus, and choose items from those menus?

• Do you know how to use My Computer, Windows Explorer, or Internet Explorer to find items stored in folders on your computer or browse the Internet?

• Are you comfortable using the mouse to move the cursor, select items, drag, and deselect? Have you used context menus, which open when you right-click items?

• When you have two or more open applications, do you know how to switch from one to another? Do you know how to switch to the Windows Desktop?

• Do you know how to open, close, and minimize individual windows? Can you move them to different locations on your screen? Can you resize a window by dragging?

• Can you scroll (vertically and horizontally) within a window to see contents that may not be visible in the displayed area?

• Are you familiar with the menus across the top of an application and how to use those menus?

• Have you used dialog boxes, such as the Print dialog box? Do you know how to click arrow icons to open a menu within a dialog box?

• Can you open, save, and close a file? Are you familiar with word processing tasks, such as typing, selecting words, backspacing, deleting, copying, pasting, and changing text?

• Do you know how to open and find information in Microsoft Windows Help?

If there are gaps in your mastery of these skills, see the Microsoft documentation for your version of Windows. Or, ask a computer-savvy friend or instructor for help.

Installing Adobe Photoshop Elements 6.0

You must purchase the Adobe Photoshop Elements 6.0 software separately and install it on a computer running Windows Vista® or Windows® XP. For system requirements and complete instructions on installing the software, see the Photoshop Elements 6.0 application CD and documentation.

Copying the Classroom in a Book files

The CD attached to the inside back cover of this book includes a Lessons folder containing all the electronic files for the lessons in this book. During the lessons, you will organize these files using a catalog that is an essential part of many projects in this book. Keep all the lesson files on your computer until after you have finished all the lessons.

Note: The files on the CD are practice files, provided for your personal use in these lessons. You are not authorized to use these files commercially, or to publish or distribute them in any form without written permission from Adobe Systems, Inc. and the individual photographers who took the pictures, or other copyright holders.

Copying the Lessons files from the CD

1   Insert the *Adobe Photoshop Elements 6.0 Classroom in a Book* CD into your CD-ROM drive. If a message appears asking what you want Windows to do, select Open folder to view files using Windows Explorer, and click OK.

If no message appears, open My Computer and double-click the CD icon to open it.

2   Locate the Lessons folder on the CD and copy it to the My Documents folder on your computer.

3   When your computer finishes copying the Lessons folder, remove the CD from your CD-ROM drive and put it away.

Go to the procedure on the next page before you start the lessons.

Creating a work folder

You'll now create a folder where you can save all of your work as you complete the lessons in this book. You'll use this folder in many of the lessons.

1   In Windows Explorer, open the Lessons folder that you copied to the My Documents folder on your hard disk.

2   In the Lessons folder, choose File > New > Folder. A new folder is created in the Lessons folder. Type **My CIB Work** to name the folder.

Creating a catalog

You'll use a catalog to organize the image files for the lessons in this book. This will keep all your images together in one easy-to-access location. You'll use the process of importing files into a catalog whenever you need to import images into Photoshop Elements from your digital camera, or import images already stored on your hard drive.

1   Start Adobe Photoshop Elements 6.0. In the Photoshop Elements Welcome Screen, click Organize in the row of shortcut buttons across the lower part of the Welcome Screen. This starts Photoshop Elements in the Organizer mode. If Photoshop Elements opens without first displaying the Welcome Screen, click the Welcome Screen button (⌂) located to the left in the menu bar to display the Welcome Screen.

Note: If this is the first time you have started the Organizer, an alert message may appear asking if you would like to specify the location of photos. Click No if this alert message appears.

2   In Photoshop Elements 6.0 (Organizer), choose File > Catalog.

3   In the Catalog Manager dialog box, click New.

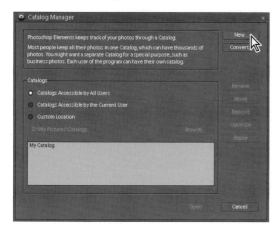

Note: Do not change the location where the Catalog file is stored.

4   In the Enter a name for the new catalog dialog box, type **CIB Catalog** as file name, deselect the Import free music into this catalog option, and then click OK.

5   In the Organizer, choose File > Get Photos and Videos > From Files and Folders. In the Get Photos from Files and Folders dialog box, open the My Documents folder. Click only once to select the Lessons folder that you copied from the CD. Do not double-click, as you do not want to open the Lessons folder.

6   Set the following options in the Get Photos from Files and Folders dialog box:

•   Confirm that the Get Photos from Subfolders checkbox is selected in the list of options above the Get Photos button.

•   Deselect the Automatically Fix Red Eyes and the Automatically Suggest Photo Stacks options. These are great options that you will learn more about as you work through the lessons, but we won't use them just yet. *(See illustration on the next page.)*

7 Click the Get Photos button. A window will open showing the photos being imported.

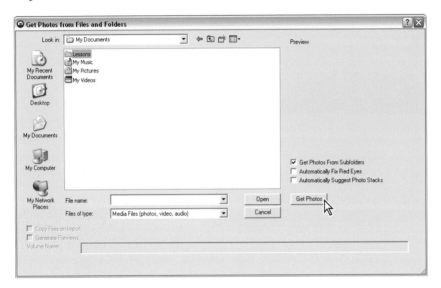

8 The Import Attached Keyword Tags dialog box opens. Click the Select All button, and then click the OK button.

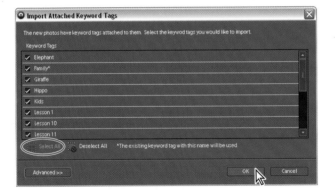

The images you are bringing into the catalog contain additional information, known as keyword tags, which will help you organize those images as you proceed through the book. We've added these keyword tags to help make it easier to work with the lessons in this book. You'll learn all about keyword tags in Lessons 2 and 3. After the image files are imported into the catalog, the imported keyword tags are available in the Keyword Tags palette. The keyword tags will be referenced in the lessons throughout this book.

9 Photoshop Elements may display a dialog box informing you that the only items displayed in the Organizer are those you just imported. If an alert is displayed, click OK to close this dialog box.

10 Click OK to close any other alert dialog box. The imported files are displayed in the Photo Browser. Use the scrollbar at the right side to browse through the images.

11 Click the Show All button above the Photo Browser.

Reconnecting missing files to a catalog

After images are added to a catalog, Adobe Photoshop Elements expects them to remain in the same location. If you move the Lessons folder or any of the files after you have created the catalog, Adobe Photoshop Elements may no longer be able to find the files. In this case, a file-missing icon (▣) on top of the image thumbnail in the Photo Browser will alert you. If there are no files missing, you can now go on to the first lesson.

Note: To avoid missing files in your catalog, use the File > Move, File > Rename, and Edit > Delete From Catalog commands in Photoshop Elements to move, rename, or delete them.

If Photoshop Elements alerts you that it cannot find an image file, you will need to carry out the following procedure to reconnect the file to your catalog.

1 Choose File > Reconnect > All Missing Files. If the message "There are no files to reconnect" appears, click OK, then skip the rest of this procedure.

2   If a message "Searching for missing files" appears, click the Browse button. The Reconnect Missing Files dialog box opens.

3   In the Browse tab on the right side of the Reconnect Missing Files dialog box, navigate to and open the moved folder.

4   Continuing to work in the Browse tab, locate and click once to select the folder that has the same name as the folder listed underneath the image thumbnail. The folder name is listed on the left side of the Reconnect Missing Files dialog box, directly under the image thumbnail.

5   After you select the appropriate folder and the correct thumbnail picture appears in the right side of the dialog box, click the Reconnect button.

6   Repeat steps 4 and 5, continuing to select the appropriate folders and clicking the Reconnect button as you find matching files. When all the files are reconnected, click the Close button.

You can now use the Photoshop Elements Organizer to select and open files in the Photoshop Elements Editor.

Note: This procedure also eliminates error messages regarding missing files when you work with Creations, or print from the Organizer.

Additional resources

Adobe Photoshop Elements 6.0 Classroom in a Book is not meant to replace documentation that comes with the program, nor is it designed to be a comprehensive reference for every feature in Photoshop Elements 6.0. For additional information about program features, refer to any of these resources:

• Photoshop Elements Help, which is built into the Adobe Photoshop Elements 6.0 application. You can view it by choosing Help > Photoshop Elements Help.

• You can also choose Help > Online Support or Help > Online Learning Resources for access to the support pages or links to additional learning resources on the Adobe Web site (www.adobe.com). Both of these options require that you have Internet access.

• The Adobe Photoshop Elements 6.0 Getting Started Guide, which is included either in the box with your copy of Adobe Photoshop Elements, or on the installation CD for the application software in PDF format. If you don't already have Adobe Reader (or if you don't have the latest version of Adobe Reader, formerly called Acrobat Reader) installed on your computer, you can download a free copy from the Adobe Web site (www.adobe.com).

Adobe Certification

The Adobe Training and Certification Programs are designed to help Adobe customers improve and promote their product-proficiency skills. The Adobe Certified Expert (ACE) program is designed to recognize the high-level skills of expert users. Adobe Certified Training Providers (ACTP) use only Adobe Certified Experts to teach Adobe software classes. Available in either ACTP classrooms or on-site, the ACE program is the best way to master Adobe products. For Adobe Certified Training Programs information, visit the Partnering with Adobe Web site at http://partners.adobe.com.

1 | A Quick Tour of Photoshop Elements

This lesson introduces the tools and the interface of Adobe Photoshop Elements 6.0. Further lessons in this book provide more in-depth exercises and specific details as to how you can take advantage of the tools.

This lesson provides an overview of the concepts and procedures involved with capturing and editing digital images using Photoshop Elements. If you prefer to skip this overview, you can jump right into working with digital images in Lesson 2. However, we encourage you to review this lesson before you get too far along in the book.

In this lesson, you will learn how to do the following:

- Work with the Organizer and the Editor.
- Attach media.
- Use the Photo Downloader.
- Review and Compare Photos.
- Send Photos in e-mail.
- Use Help and the How To palette.

How Photoshop Elements works

About workspaces

Photoshop Elements has two primary workspaces: the Organizer for finding, organizing and sharing photos and media files, and the Editor for creating, editing and fixing your images.

When a photo is selected in the Organizer, clicking the Editor button (✐) located near the top right corner of the Organizer window, and then choosing Quick Fix, Full Edit, or Guided Edit from the menu, opens the selected photo in the Editor workspace. In the Editor, clicking the Organizer button (▦) located near the top right corner of the Editor window opens the Organizer workspace.

Use the buttons at the top of the work area to switch between the Organizer (shown in the background in the above illustration) and the Editor (shown in the foreground in the above illustration).

💡 *Once both the Organizer and the Editor are open in Photoshop Elements, you can also move between the two workspaces by clicking the corresponding button in the Windows task bar at the bottom of the screen.*

The Organizer workspace

The Organizer lets you find, organize and share your photos and media files in the Photo Browser. It can display a single photo or media file, or display thumbnails of all the photos and media files in your catalog. If you prefer viewing your photos and media files by date, the Organizer has a Date View workspace that lets you work with your files in a calendar format.

The Photo Browser lists all the photos and cataloged assets in one comprehensive window that you can easily browse through. It can show previews of files stored remotely, such as on a CD.

In the Organize panel of the Task pane, organize your photos by using keyword tags and by placing them in albums.

The Fix panel of the Task pane offers tools for the most common photographic editing tasks, such as color correction and red eye removal. For more complex editing tasks, selecting Quick Fix, Full Edit, or Guided Edit switches to the Editor workspace.

Use the Create panel of the Task pane to create projects such as greeting cards or slide shows, and use the tools in the Share panel to share your files with others.

The Editor workspace

The Editor lets you focus on creating and editing images. Depending on your needs, you can choose between the Full Edit workspace with tools to correct color, create special effects, or enhance photos, the Quick Fix workspace with simple tools and commands to quickly fix common problems, and the Guided Edit workspace with step-by-step instructions for common editing tasks.

If you are new to digital imaging, Quick Fix or Guided Edit is a good place to start fixing photos.

If you've previously worked with image editing software, you'll find that the Full Edit workspace provides a more flexible and powerful image editing environment. This function has lighting and color correction commands, tools to fix image imperfections, selection tools, text editing tools and painting tools. You can arrange the Full Edit workspace to best suit your needs by moving, hiding and showing palettes, arranging palettes in the Palette Bin, zooming in or out of a photo, scrolling to a different area of the document window and creating multiple windows and views.

The Full Edit workspace.

Using the Palette Bin

The Palette Bin of the Full Edit workspace provides a convenient location to store and manage the palettes you use for editing images. By default, only the Effects and Layers palettes are placed in the Palette Bin. Other palettes that you open (using the Window menu) are positioned in the work area. These are known as floating palettes. You can change which palettes float and which are stored in the Palette Bin.

To add floating palettes to the Palette Bin

1 Choose Window > [palette name] to open the palette you want to place in the Palette Bin.

2 Drag the palette by its tab to the Palette Bin. The tab contains the palette name. To reposition the palette without placing it in the Palette Bin, drag the palette by the bar across the top of the palette.

You can also choose the Place in Palette Bin when Closed option from the palette menu, and then close the palette window.

To remove palettes from the Palette Bin or close palettes:

1 Drag a palette out of the Palette Bin by clicking and dragging the title bar that lists the name of the palette.

2 Click the palette menu and deselect Place in Palette Bin when Closed option.

3 To close a palette, choose Window > [palette name], or click the close box (✖) in the top right corner of a floating palette. Palettes that display a check mark adjacent to their name in the Window menu are visible; selecting a palette name that includes a check mark causes the palette window to close.

To adjust palette sizes in the Palette Bin

Adjust the height of palettes by doing either or both of the following:

• Click the triangle to the left of the palette bin to adjust the palette bin width.

• Click and drag the separator bars between palettes up or down to adjust the height of a palette.

Workflow

The fundamental workflow for Adobe Photoshop Elements is to:

- Capture images and media into the Organizer from a digital camera, scanner, or digital video camera.

- Organize images and media—including applying keyword tags—using the Organizer.

- Edit images and media by color correcting or adding text, using the Editor.

- Share images and media by e-mailing, using a sharing service, or burning to CD/DVD ROM.

Attaching media

Importing digital files directly into Photoshop Elements is easy.

Getting photos

To view and organize your photos in Photoshop Elements, you first need to bring them into the application. You can get photos into Photoshop Elements in several ways:

- Bring photos from your camera or card reader directly into the Photoshop Elements Organizer using Adobe Photo Downloader. Getting photos directly will save you time and enable you to quickly start working with your photos.

• Use the software that came with your digital camera to download pictures to your computer, and then bring them into Photoshop Elements using the From Files and Folders command. If you prefer to work with other software to import your files to your computer, you'll need to disable Adobe Photo Downloader to use the other software. To disable the Adobe Photo Downloader, click its icon (📷) in the system tray or task bar, and then choose Disable. Only do this if you plan to use other software to bring images onto your computer.

• If your camera or card reader displays as a drive, e.g., in My Computer, you can drag the files to a folder on your hard drive, and then bring them into Photoshop Elements using the From Files and Folders command.

In most cases, you'll need to install software drivers that came with your camera before you can download pictures to your computer. You may also need to set up the Photoshop Elements Camera or Card Reader Preferences. See "Getting photos" in Lesson 2, "Basic Organizing."

Creating a new catalog

You organize your photographs in catalogs, which manage the image files on your computer but are independent of the photo files themselves. Along with digital photographs, you can include in a catalog video and audio files, scans, PDF documents, and other personal creations. A single catalog can efficiently handle thousands of files, but you can also create separate catalogs for different types of work.

1 Start Photoshop Elements, either by double-clicking the shortcut on your desktop or by choosing Start > All Programs > Adobe Photoshop Elements 6.0.

2 Do one of the following:

• If the Welcome Screen appears, click Organize in the row of shortcut buttons across the lower part of the Welcome Screen. Wait until the Organizer has finished opening.

• If Photoshop Elements 6.0 (Editor) opens without first displaying the Welcome Screen, click the Welcome Screen button (🏠) located to the left in the menu bar to display the Welcome Screen, and then click Organize. Or, click the Organizer button (⊞) located to the right in the menu bar. Wait until the Organizer has finished opening.

• If Photoshop Elements 6.0 (Organizer) opens, you are ready to continue with step 3.

3 In Organizer mode, choose File > Catalog.

4   In the Catalog Manager dialog box, click New.

5   In the Enter a name for the new catalog dialog box, type **Lesson1** as file name, deselect the Import free music into this catalog option, and then click OK.

Now you have a special catalog that you'll use just for this lesson. All you need is some pictures to put in it.

Using the Adobe Photo Downloader

For the rest of this lesson you will need to import images into the Organizer. If you have a digital camera and images of your own, follow the steps in the next section. Otherwise, skip to the section, "To get photos from files and folders."

Getting photos from a digital camera or card reader

You can import files from your camera directly into Photoshop Elements.

1   Connect your camera or card reader to your computer. For instructions on connecting your device, see the documentation that came with it.

2 Do the following:

• If the Windows Auto Play dialog box appears, click Cancel.

• If the Photo Downloader dialog box appears automatically, continue with step 3.

• If the Photo Downloader dialog box does not appear automatically, choose File > Get Photos and Videos > From Camera or Card Reader.

3 Under Source in the Photo Downloader dialog box, choose the name of the connected camera or card reader from the Get Photos from menu.

4 Under Import Settings, accept the folder location listed next to Location, or click Browse to choose a new location for the files.

5 Next to Create Subfolder(s), choose one of the date formats if you want the photos to be stored in a folder whose name includes the date the photos were imported or taken. You can also choose Custom Name to create a folder using a name you type in the text box, or choose None if you don't want to create any subfolder. Your selection is reflected in the pathname displayed next to Location.

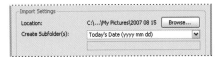

6   Choose Do not rename files from the Rename Files menu, and from the Delete Options menu choose After Copying, Do Not Delete Originals. If selected, deselect the Automatic Download check box.

You will learn more about customizing import settings and the advanced features of the Adobe Photo Downloader in Lessons 2 and 3.

7   Click the Get Photos button.

The photos are copied from the camera to the specified folder location.

8   If the Files Successfully Copied dialog box appears, click OK.

The Getting Photos dialog box appears and the photos are imported into Photoshop Elements.

If the imported photos contain keyword metadata, the Import Attached Keyword Tags dialog box appears. Select the keyword tags you want to import. The keyword tags you select are added to the Keyword Tags palette when the photos are imported. If a keyword tag has an asterisk (*), you already have a keyword tag of the same name in your catalog and that keyword tag is attached to the photos.

9   Click OK to close any other alert dialog box.

The imported photos appear in the Photo Browser.

About keyword tags

Keyword tags are personalized labels, such as "Vacation" or "Beach," that you attach to photos, video clips, audio clips and other creations in the Photo Browser to easily organize and find them. When you use keyword tags, there's no need to manually organize your photos in subject-specific folders or rename files with content-specific names. Instead, you simply attach one or more keyword tags to each photo. You can then easily retrieve the photos you want by clicking the appropriate keyword tags in the Keyword Tags palette.

For example, you can create a keyword tag called "Christine" and attach it to every photo featuring your sister, Christine. You can then instantly find all the photos with the Christine keyword tag by clicking the Find box next to the Christine keyword tag in the Keyword Tags palette, regardless of where the photos are stored on your computer.

You can create keyword tags using any labels you want. For instance, you can create keyword tags for individual people, places and events in your life. You can attach multiple keyword tags to your photos. When photos have multiple keyword tags, you can easily run a search on a combination of keyword tags to find a particular person at a particular place or event. For example, you can search for all "Christine" keyword tags and all "John" keyword tags to find all pictures of Christine with her husband, John. Or search for all "Christine" keyword tags and all "California" keyword tags to find all the pictures of Christine vacationing in California.

Use keyword tags to organize and find photos by their content. You specify names for your keyword tags and choose the photos that fall into those categories. See Lessons 2 and 3 for more information on keyword tags.

Getting photos from files and folders

Digital images stored on your computer can also be imported into Photoshop Elements.

1	Choose File > Get Photos and Videos > From Files and Folders.

2	In the Get Photos dialog box, navigate to the Lesson01 folder and click once to select the Photos folder that contains sample images.

3	Select the Get Photos From Subfolders check box. If selected, deselect the Automatically Fix Red Eyes and the Automatically Suggest Photo Stacks check boxes, and then click Get Photos.

The Getting Photos dialog box appears and the photos are imported into Photoshop Elements. Since the imported photos contain keyword metadata, the Import Attached Keyword Tags dialog box appears. You will learn more about keyword tags in Lessons 2 and 3.

4	In the Import Attached Keyword Tags dialog box, click Select All, and then click OK. Click OK to close any other alert dialog box.

The imported photos appear in the Organizer.

Reviewing and comparing

Photoshop Elements provides several options to quickly and easily review and compare images.

Viewing photos at full screen or side-by-side

The Full Screen View and Side by Side View let you review your images without the distraction of other interface items such as windows, menus and palettes.

1   Click the Display button (◼) near the upper right corner of the Organizer window, and then choose View Photos in Full Screen from the menu.

In the Full Screen View Options dialog box, you can customize the slide show—for example, you can play an audio file as you view the images. You can also choose to display thumbnails of the selected files in a filmstrip along the right side of the screen, or add a fade between pictures.

2   Deselect Include Captions and select Start Playing Automatically. Then, click OK to start the slide show.

Your photos are displayed as a full-screen slide show, making it a fun and efficient way to view a set of photos.

The control bar, which contains buttons for playing, rotating and zooming disappears from view when you don't move the mouse for a couple of seconds.

3   To make the control bar reappear, move the mouse.

When you view images in full screen, you can quickly assign a rating. On the right end of the control bar, click a star to apply a rating. You can also apply the rating using the shortcut keys, 1 (for 1 star) through 5 (for 5 stars).

4   Press the Esc key on your keyboard to return to the Organizer.

5   Click the Display button (▪), and then choose Compare Photos Side by Side to display two photos simultaneously. Side by Side View is useful when you need to focus on details and differences between photos. You can select two or more photos to compare. When you click the Next Photo button (●) in the control bar, the selected image changes to the next image in your catalog. By default, image # 1 (on the left or top) is selected. To select image #2 instead, click it.

Note: *The selected image has a blue border. If you have the filmstrip showing, you can click any image in the filmstrip to view it in place of the selected image.*

Use Side by Side View to analyze composition and details.

You can switch between views by clicking the Full Screen View button (▣) or the Side by Side View button (▣▣) in the control bar. While in either view, you can right-click an image and access further options from the context menu. You can, for example, mark an image for printing, fix red eye, add a photo to an album, and delete or apply keyword tags.

6　Press the Esc key on your keyboard to return to the Organizer.

💡 *Choose the photos to be compared in the Organizer by holding the Ctrl key and selecting the images. Then, choose View > Compare Photos Side by Side.*

Choosing files

To select more than one photo in the Photo Browser, hold down the Ctrl key and click the photos you want to select. Holding down the Ctrl key enables you to select multiple, non-consecutive files. To select photos that are in consecutive order, click the first photo, and then hold down the Shift key and click the last photo you want. All the photos between the first and last photos will be selected as well.

Sharing photos in e-mail

Have you ever had to wait long time for an incoming e-mail to download, and then find that the e-mail contained only a single photograph in an unnecessarily high resolution? You can avoid imposing this inconvenience on others by using the Organizer e-mail function, which creates a version of the image that is optimized specifically for sending via e-mail.

1　In the Photo Browser, select the photo (or photos) you'd like to send in an e-mail.

2　In the Share panel of the Task pane, click the E-mail Attachments button.

Note: When you use this function for the first time, you are asked to select the e-mail service you want to use. You can later review or change your settings under Edit > Preferences > Sharing.

3   (Optional) Drag photos from the Photo Browser to add to your selection.

4   Select Very Small (320 x 240 px) from the Maximum Photo Size menu and adjust the image quality using the Quality slider (the higher the quality the larger the file size and the longer the download time). The resulting file size and download time for a typical 56 Kbps dial-up modem are estimated and displayed for your reference. When done, click Next.

5 Under Message, select and delete the "Here are the photos...." text and type a message of your own.

6 Next to Select Recipients, click the Edit Contact Book button (👤). In the Contact Book dialog box, click the New Contact button (👤). In the New Contact dialog box, type in the name (or a nickname—our example uses Mom) of the person to whom you want to send the picture, and that person's e-mail address. Click OK to close the New Contact dialog box and click OK again to close the Contact Book dialog box.

7 Under Select Recipients, click the check box next to Mom to select it, and then click Next.

Your default e-mail application immediately creates an e-mail message. You can edit the message and Subject line to say what you want. When you are finished and ready to send the e-mail, then either make sure that you are connected to the Internet and click Send if you want to send an actual e-mail, or close the message without saving or sending it.

8 Switch back to Photoshop Elements (Organizer).

Using Help

Help is available in several ways, each one useful to you for different circumstances:

Help in the application The complete documentation for using Adobe Photoshop Elements is available as Help in the application, which is HTML content you access through your default browser, such as Internet Explorer. Help in the application provides easy access to summarized information on common tasks and concepts. Help in the application can be especially useful if you are new to Photoshop Elements or if you aren't connected to the Internet.

LiveDocs Help on the Web This is the most comprehensive and up-to-date version of Photoshop Elements Help. It is the recommended choice if you have an active Internet connection.

Note: You do not need to be connected to the Internet to view Help in the application. However, with an active Internet connection, clicking the "This page on the Web" link on any page in the application's Help opens the corresponding page in LiveDocs.

Help PDF Help is also available as a PDF that is optimized for printing; just go to http://www.adobe.com/go/learn_pse_printpdf to download the PDF document.

Note: The Help PDF file is about 36 MBytes in size and may take a considerable time to download when using a slow Internet connection.

Links in the application Within the Photoshop Elements application there are links to additional help topics, such as the "Tell me more" link at the bottom of the panel in each guided task.

Navigating Help in the application

Choose Help > Photoshop Elements Help, or press the F1 key. Your default Web browser will open and display the starting page of the Adobe Photoshop Help in the application. Do any of the following:

• Select Contents in the top left corner of the window. Click a topic heading in the table of content on the left side of the window. Click the plus sign (+) to the left of a topic heading to see its sub-topics. Select a topic or sub-topic to display its content on the right side of the window.

• Select Contents in the top left corner of the window. Click on a letter to display index entries starting with that letter. Click the plus sign (+) to the left of an index header or click the index header to see its entries. Click the index entry to display its content on the right side of the window.

• Select Search in the top left corner of the window. Enter a search term, and then click Search. When the search has finished, click a search result in the list on the left side of the window to display its content on the right side of the window.

Search tips

Adobe Help Search works by searching the entire Help text for topics that contain all the words typed in the Search box. These tips can help you improve your search results in Help:

• If you search using a phrase, such as "shape tool," put quotation marks around the phrase. The search returns only those topics containing that specific phrase.

• Make sure that the search terms are spelled correctly.

• If a search term doesn't yield results, try using a synonym, such as "photo" instead of "picture."

Accessing LiveDocs Help on the Web

LiveDocs Help on the Web contains the most up-to-date version of Photoshop Elements Help. In addition, it enables you to search across multiple applications.

1 To access Photoshop Elements' LiveDocs Help on the Web, part of the Adobe Help Resource Center, do any of the following:

• Click the "This page on the Web" link, located at the bottom of any topic page in Adobe Help in the application.

• In your Web browser, open the Adobe Help Resource Center at http://www.adobe.com/support/documentation. Select Photoshop Elements from the list of products, and then click Go. On the Photoshop Elements resources page, click the LiveDocs link.

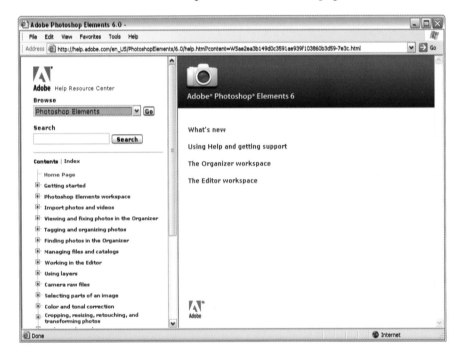

2 To switch to LiveDocs Help for a different product, select that product from the list under Browse, and then click Go.

3 To search for a topic, enter the search term under Search, and then click Search. To search across all products, select Search all products on the LiveDocs Search Results page, enter the search term, and then click Go.

Links to help in the application

There are some links to additional help within the Photoshop Elements application. Clicking these links will take you to the corresponding topic in either Help in the application or LiveDocs Help on the Web.

Hot-linked tips

Hot-linked tips are available throughout Adobe Photoshop Elements. These tips display information in the form of a typical tip balloon, or they will link you to the appropriate topic in the help file.

You've reached the end of the first lesson. Now that you understand how to get photos and the essentials of the Photoshop Elements interface, you are ready to start organizing and editing photos—which you'll do in the next lessons.

Review

▶ **Review questions**

1 What are the primary workspaces in Adobe Photoshop Elements 6.0?

2 Define the fundamental workflow.

3 What is the function of a catalog?

4 What are keyword tags?

5 How can you select multiple thumbnail images in the Photo Browser?

▶ **Review answers**

1 Photoshop Elements has two main workspaces: the Organizer workspace for finding, organizing and sharing photos and media files, and the Editor workspace for creating, editing and fixing your images. You can use the buttons on the top of the work area to switch between the Organizer and the Editor.

2 The fundamental workflow in Adobe Photoshop Elements involves:

a Capturing media into the Organizer from a digital camera, scanner, digital video camera, or an image created from scratch in the editing component.

b Categorize the media in the Organizer using the tag assignment features.

c Edit the media by color correcting or adding text, using the Editor.

d Share the media by e-mailing, using a sharing service or burning to CD/DVD ROM.

3 You organize your photographs in catalogs that manage the image files on your computer but are independent of the photo files themselves. Along with digital photographs, you can include video and audio files, scans, PDF documents, and your personal creations in a catalog. A single catalog can efficiently handle thousands of photos, but to better manage your image files you can also create separate catalogs for different types of work.

4 Keyword tags are personalized labels such as "House" or "Beach" that you attach to photos, creations, and video or audio clips in the Photo Browser so that you can easily organize and find them.

5   To select more than one photo in the Photo Browser, hold down the Ctrl key and click the photos you want to select. Holding down the Ctrl key enables you to select multiple, non-consecutive files. To select photos that are in consecutive order, click the first photo, hold down the Shift key, and then click the last photo you want. All the photos between the first and last photos will be selected as well.

2 | Basic Organizing

After capturing your memories with your digital camera, you'll want to store and organize your pictures on your computer. This lesson gets you started with the essential skills you'll need to import and track your images.

In this lesson, you will learn how to do the following:

- Open Adobe Photoshop Elements 6.0 in Organizer mode.

- Create a catalog of your images.

- Import images into a catalog from a digital camera or from folders on your computer.

- Change the display of thumbnails in your Photo Browser.

- Create, organize, and apply tags to images.

Photoshop Elements 6.0 for Windows includes two primary parts: the Editor and the Organizer. Together they work hand-in-hand to help you find, share, and make corrections to your photographs and images.

Before you start working in Adobe Photoshop Elements 6.0, make sure that you have installed the software on your computer from the application CD. See "Installing Adobe Photoshop Elements 6.0" on page 3.

Also make sure that you have correctly copied the Lessons folder from the CD in the back of this book onto your computer's hard disk. See "Copying the Classroom in a Book files" on page 3.

Most people need between one and two hours to complete all the projects in this lesson.

Getting started

In this lesson, you're going to work primarily in the Organizer component of Photoshop Elements.

1   Start Photoshop Elements, either by double-clicking the shortcut on your desktop, or by choosing Start > All Programs > Adobe Photoshop Elements 6.0.

2   Do one of the following:

•   If the Welcome Screen appears, click Organize in the row of shortcut buttons across the lower part of the Welcome Screen.

•   If Photoshop Elements 6.0 (Editor) opens without first displaying the Welcome Screen, click the Welcome Screen button (⌂) located to the left in the menu bar to display the Welcome Screen, and then click Organize. Or, click the Organizer button (▦) located to the right in the menu bar. Then, wait until the Organizer has finished opening.

•   If Photoshop Elements 6.0 (Organizer) opens, you don't have to do anything more and are all set to start with this lesson.

💡 *From the menu located in the lower left corner of the Welcome Screen, you can choose to either display the Welcome Screen next time you start Photoshop Elements, or not to display the Welcome Screen and instead open directly in the Editor or Organizer.*

Getting photos

The Organizer component of Photoshop Elements gives you a working area where you can efficiently organize, sort, and perform basic editing of your pictures. When you want to print your photographs or send them with an e-mail, having the images collected in the Organizer is an essential step in the process, as you'll see later in this lesson.

Creating a new catalog

Photoshop Elements organizes your photographs in catalogs that enable you to manage the image files on your computer. Catalogs are independent of the photo files themselves. You can include video and audio files along with digital photographs and scans in your catalogs. A single catalog can efficiently handle thousands of photos, but you can also create separate catalogs for different types of work. You'll create a new catalog now so that you won't confuse the practice files for this lesson with the other lesson files for this book.

Note: In this book, the forward arrow character (>) is used to refer to commands and submenus found in the menus at the top of the application window, for example, File, Edit, and so forth.

1   In Photoshop Elements 6.0 (Organizer), choose File > Catalog.

2   In the Catalog Manager dialog box, click New.

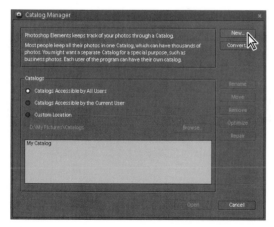

3 In the Enter a name for the new catalog dialog box, type **Lesson2** as file name, deselect the Import free music into this catalog option, and then click OK.

You will use this catalog to import—by various methods—the images for this lesson.

Dragging photos from Windows Explorer

This method of adding photographs to an Organizer catalog, using the familiar drag-and-drop technique, couldn't be easier or more intuitive.

1 Minimize the Organizer by clicking the Minimize button (▫) towards the right end of the menu bar, or by clicking the Organizer application button on the Windows taskbar.

2 Open My Computer by whatever method you usually use, such as double-clicking an icon on the desktop, using the Start menu, or using Windows Explorer.

3 Navigate through the folder structure to find and open the Lesson02 folder you copied to your hard disk (see "Copying the Classroom in a Book files" on page 3). You'll see three folders inside the Lesson02 folder: BATCH1, BATCH2, and BATCH3.

4 Drag and hold the BATCH1 folder icon over the Organizer application button on the Windows taskbar.

5 Wait until the Organizer becomes the foreground application, and then drag and release the pointer with the BATCH1 folder icon in the Organizer application window.

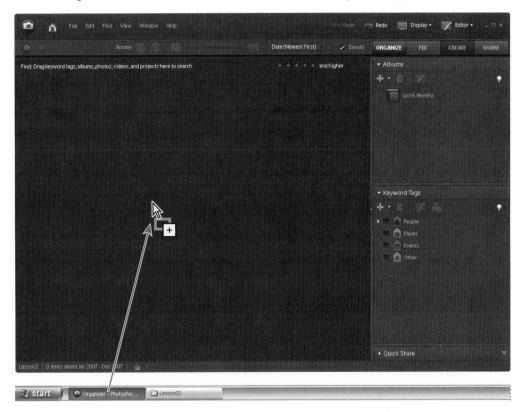

💡 *If you can arrange the Windows Explorer window and the Organizer application window on your screen so that you can see both windows at the same time, you can also drag and drop the folder icon (or individual files) directly from the Windows Explorer window onto the Organizer application window.*

The Organizer will briefly display a dialog box while searching inside the BATCH1 folder for files to import.

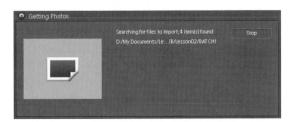

Because the files found in the BATCH1 folder have keyword tags applied to them to help keep them organized, the Import Attached Keyword Tags dialog box will open.

6   In the Import Attached Keyword Tags dialog box, click Select All, and then click OK.

You will briefly see the Getting Photos dialog box while the Organizer is importing the image files from the BATCH1 folder.

7   If a message appears telling you that only the newly imported items will be visible in the main window of the catalog, click OK.

💡 *If you don't want to see this message each time you import new items, select Don't Show Again before clicking OK. To have it show again, click Reset All Warning Dialogs in the General section of the Preferences dialog box.*

8   Click the Maximize button (▣) towards the right end of the menu bar in the Organizer window. This causes the window to expand and cover the entire screen.

In the Photo Browser, you can now see thumbnails of the four images you've added to your Lesson2 catalog. Don't drag the other two batches into the Organizer because you're going to use different methods of adding them to your catalog.

> 💡 *The timeline above the Photo Browser that you might be familiar with from earlier versions of Photoshop Elements, is now hidden by default. To toggle the visibility of the timeline, choose Window > Timeline. To customize the amount of information displayed in the Photo Browser, select or deselect View > Details. With View > Details selected, you can additionally select or deselect View > Show File Names, or View > Show Grid Lines. Another option is to select or deselect View > Show Borders around Thumbnails.*

Getting photos from specific locations

A second technique for adding items to your catalog is to use a menu command instead of having to resize and arrange windows on the desktop.

1   Choose File > Get Photos and Videos > From Files and Folders.

2   In the Get Photos from Files and Folders dialog box, navigate to the Lesson02 folder and open the BATCH2 folder.

3   One by one, hover (don't click!) with the pointer over each of the four image files inside the BATCH2 folder. You'll see additional information about the image next to the pointer, and a thumbnail image is displayed in the Preview area.

4   If selected, deselect the Automatically Fix Red Eyes and the Automatically Suggest Photo Stacks check boxes.

5   Press Ctrl+A, or drag-select the four images in the BATCH2 folder, and then click the Get Photos button.

> Select a folder icon in the Get Photos from Files and Folders dialog box, and then click Get Photos to import all items within that folder (and its subfolders if the Get Photos From Subfolders check box is selected).

6   In the Import Attached Keyword Tags dialog box, notice that the keyword tag "Lesson 2" from the new batch of images will, if selected, map to the existing keyword tag in the catalog (from the import of the images in the first batch). Click the Advanced button in the lower left corner of the dialog box. Here you could assign a new name to keyword tags found in the imported items, or map them to other existing keyword tags in the catalog. But for now, leave things unchanged and just click the Reset to Basic button.

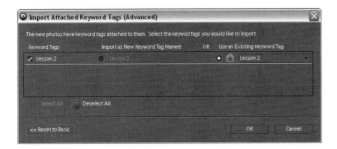

7   Click Select All, and then click OK. To close any other alert dialog box, click OK.

8   Click the Show All button above the Photo Browser to see all eight images.

9   To rotate the last image of the second batch, named 02_08.jpg, click to select it, and then click the Rotate Left button (⬑) above the Photo Browser.

Automatically Fixing Red Eyes

The term "red eye" refers to the often-observed phenomenon in photos taken with a flash, where the subject's irises are red instead of black. This is caused by the flash reflecting off the back of the eye.

While none of the images in this lesson require red eye correction, when needed you can quickly remove red eye automatically while importing images into the Photo Browser. To remove red eye automatically, select the Automatically Fix Red Eyes check box in the Get Photos from Files and Folders dialog box.

Additional ways to fix red eye will be discussed in lessons 3 and 6.

Searching for photos to add

This method is probably the one you'll want to use if you're not sure where in your folder structure you've stashed photographs and other resources over the years. Ordinarily, you might run this search on your entire hard disk or for the whole My Documents folder. For this demonstration, you'll limit your search area to a very restricted part of the folder organization on your computer.

1   In the Organizer, choose File > Get Photos and Videos > By Searching.

2   Under Search Options in the Get Photos By Searching for Folders dialog box, choose Browse from the Look In menu.

3   In the Browse For Folder dialog box, click to select the Lesson02 folder, and then click OK.

4   Under Search Options in the Get Photos By Searching for Folders dialog box, deselect the Automatically Fix Red Eyes check box, if not already deselected.

5   Click the Search button located in the upper right corner of the dialog box.

6   Under Search Results, click to select only the BATCH3 folder, and then click the Import Folders button.

7   In the Import Attached Keyword Tags dialog box, click Select All, and then click OK. Click OK to close any other alert dialog box. In the Organizer, examine the newly imported items, and then click the Show All button above the Photo Browser to see all 12 images now in your Lesson2 catalog.

Importing from a digital camera

This exercise is optional and requires that you have an available digital camera or memory card from your camera with pictures on it. You can either perform this procedure now, or skip to the Viewing photo thumbnails section later in this lesson.

1 Connect your digital camera or the card reader for your digital camera to your computer, following the equipment manufacturer's instructions.

2 Do the following:

• If the Windows Auto Play dialog box appears, click Cancel.

• If the Photo Downloader dialog box appears automatically, continue with step 3.

• If the Photo Downloader dialog box does not appear automatically, choose File > Get Photos and Videos > From Camera or Card Reader.

> *You can also launch the Adobe Photo Downloader by double-clicking its icon ( ) in the system tray in the lower right corner of your screen.*

3 Under Source in the Photo Downloader dialog box, choose from the Get Photos from menu the name of the connected camera or card reader.

4   Under Import Settings, accept the folder location listed next to Location, or click Browse to choose a new location for the files.

5   Next to Create Subfolder(s), choose Today's Date (yyyy mm dd) as folder name format from the menu. Your selection is reflected in the pathname displayed next to Location.

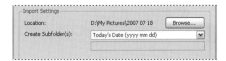

6   Choose Do not rename files from the Rename Files menu, and from the Delete Options menu choose After Copying, Do Not Delete Originals. If selected, deselect the Automatic Download check box.

7   Click the Advanced Dialog button.

Thumbnail images of the photos in your camera's memory card appear in the Advanced Dialog of the Photo Downloader.

8 (Optional) Click the check box (removing the green check mark), to remove photos from the import list. Unselected images are not imported.

Note: If you choose to delete the originals after copying under Advanced Options, only images actually imported will be deleted from the camera.

9 (Optional) Select one or more photos to rotate. Click the Rotate Left button or the Rotate Right button located in the lower left corner of the dialog box:

10 Under Advanced Options, if selected, deselect the three check boxes for Automatically Fix Red Eyes, Automatically Suggest Photo Stacks, and Make 'Group Custom Name' as a Tag. Then, click Get Photos.

The selected photos are copied from the camera to the specified folder on your hard disk.

11 If the Files Successfully Copied dialog box appears, click OK.

The Getting Photos dialog box appears and the photos are imported into Photoshop Elements.

12 Click OK to close any other alert dialog box.

The imported photos appear in the Photo Browser, already rotated where specified.

Using watched folders

Watched folders are folders on your computer that automatically alert Photoshop Elements when a new photo is saved or added to the folder. By default, the My Pictures folder is watched, but you can add additional folders to the list. New images added to these folders can be automatically added to the Organizer.

You can set up watched folders in two ways. You can choose to have new photos that are detected in a watched folder automatically added to your catalog, or you can opt to be asked before photos are added. When you choose this option, the message "New files have been found in Watched Folders" appears when new photos are detected. Just click Yes to add the photos to your catalog, or click No to skip them.

Now you'll add a folder to the watched folders list.

1   Choose File > Watch Folders.

2   Under Folders to Watch in the Watch Folders dialog box, click Add, and then browse to the Lesson02 folder.

3   Select the Lesson02 folder, and then click OK.

The folder name appears in the Folders to Watch list. To delete a folder name from that list, select its name, and then click Remove.

4   Keep the Notify Me option selected, and then click OK to close the Watch Folders dialog box.

Note: In Lesson 3, which talks about advanced organizing, you will find more ways of getting pictures.

Viewing photo thumbnails in the Organizer

There are several ways to view your Organizer catalog. While some display preferences let you change the display to meet your needs, other options can make it easier to work with items in the Organizer.

Using Photo Browser view

Up to this point, you've been working in the default Photo Browser view, the Thumbnail View. The Organizer also has other options for displaying images.

1 Click the Display button (■) near the upper right corner of the Organizer window, and then choose Import Batch from the menu to see the thumbnails organized by their separate import sessions.

Notice the bar and film canister icons (■) separating each row of thumbnails.

2 Try the following:

• Click the separator bar between two batches (reading "Imported from hard disk on ...") to select the thumbnails of all images imported in that session.

• Change the thumbnail size by dragging the slider above the Photo Browser.

• Choose Window > Timeline if the timeline is not currently visible above the Photo Browser. Click one of the three bars in the timeline to jump to the first image imported in that session.

The view switches to the first image in that batch, the date for that image flashes off and on, and a green border temporarily surrounds the image.

3   Before you continue, reduce the thumbnail size if necessary, making it small enough so that you can see all the images in your catalog.

4   Using the Display menu that you used in Step 1, select Folder Location to see the thumbnails organized according to the folders in which they are stored on your computer.

5　Repeat the same steps you performed in Step 2.

6　Select one of the bars in the timeline above the Photo Browser to jump to the photographs taken at the selected point in the timeline.

Note: *To display the file name of individual images in the Browser View, make sure View > Details is selected, and then choose View > Show File Names.*

Using Date View

Particularly if you are working with a collection of pictures that span a number of years, Date View is a great way to organize your images.

1　Click the Display button (▣) near the upper right corner of the Organizer window, and then choose Date View from the menu.

2　Select the Year option under the calendar display (bottom center left), if it is not already selected. Use the right and left arrows on either side of the year heading in the calendar to go to 2007, if it is not already selected.

3　Select June 30 on the 2007 calendar.

A preview of the first photograph taken on June 30, 2007, appears on the right.

4   Under the thumbnail image on the right side of the Organizer window, click the Next Item On Selected Day button (⊙) repeatedly to see the other photographs taken on the same day.

💡 *You can also click the Start Automatic Sequencing button (⊙) to view all photos of the selected day as a slide show.*

5   Under the thumbnail image to the right, click the Find this photo in the Photo Browser button (👥) to switch to the Photo Browser with the current photo highlighted.

6   In the Photo Browser, click the Back to previous view button (◀) near the upper left corner of the Organizer window to return to the Date View.

7 Select the Month option under the calendar display.

8 Using the date at the top of the calendar, click the word June, and then choose July from the menu of months that appears. You can use this method to quickly jump to a specific month. In this case a simple click on the Next Month button would have done the trick as well.

9 Click in the Daily Note area (bottom right) and type **A grand day out** to add a note to the date.

Now that you know how to locate your images in Date View, you can reset the Organizer to your preferred settings whenever you want to. For these lessons, you'll go back to Photo Browser rather than Date View.

Working with star ratings and keyword tags

Most of us find it challenging to organize our files and folders efficiently. Forgetting which pictures were stored in what folder is easy, and it's tedious to have to open and examine the contents of numerous folders looking for images or files.

The good news is that such searches are a thing of the past. You saw earlier how you can use the Search feature in the Organizer to find and import files from multiple locations on your computer. The next set of topics will show you how a little time invested in applying star ratings and keyword tags can streamline the process of sorting through your pictures, regardless of where the image files are stored.

Applying keyword tags and rating photos

Keyword tags and keyword tag categories are search criteria that you apply to images. You can also rate photos—applying one to five stars— and choose to display items based on their assigned rating. In this example, you'll apply a rating and a couple of keyword tags from the default set to one of the images you imported into your catalog.

1   Click the Display button (■), and then choose Thumbnail View from the menu.

2   In the Photo Browser, hover (don't click yet!) with the pointer over the stars underneath a thumbnail image of your choice. When the number of yellow stars you'd like to assign to this image is selected, click to apply that rating.

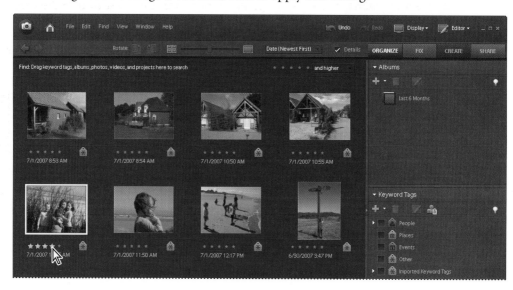

Using Star rating and the Hidden tags

Star rating—Use *Star rating* to rank you photos. You can attach only one star rating value per photo. If you assign 5 stars to a photo that already has 4 stars assigned, the 5 stars replace the 4 stars.

Hidden—The *Hidden tag* hides photos in the Photo Browser, unless you select the Hidden tag as search criteria. Use the Hidden tag, for example, to hide items that you want to keep, but generally don't want to see.

—From Photoshop Elements Help

3   Find images based on their assigned rating using the stars and the menu located above the Photo Browser.

4   Click the Show All button.

5   Under Keyword Tags in the Organize panel, click the arrow next to the People category to expand it so that you can see the Family and Friends sub-categories.

6   Drag the Family sub-category tag to the thumbnail showing the four children at the beach.

7   Allow the cursor to rest for a few seconds over the keyword tag icons under each thumbnail image until a tip appears, identifying the keyword tags that are applied to the image.

Creating new categories and sub-categories

You can add or delete new keyword tag categories and sub-categories to meet your needs.

1 Under Keyword Tags in the Organize pane, click the Create New button (✛) and choose New Category from the menu.

2 In the Create Category dialog box, type **Nature**, and select the flower symbol under Category Icon. You may have to scroll to the right to see the flower symbol. Click OK.

3 Under Keyword Tags, click to select the People category, and then click the Create New button (✛) and choose New Sub-Category.

4 In the Create Sub-Category dialog box, type **Kids** in the Sub-Category Name field. Make sure that People is shown in the Parent Category or Sub-Category field, and then click OK.

The new keyword tag category and sub-category become part of this catalog.

Applying and editing category assignments

You can add keyword tags to several files at once, and—or course—remove keyword tag assignments.

1   In the Photo Browser, click to select a picture with a child. Then, press and hold the Ctrl key and click all other kid pictures to select them, too. You should have multiple pictures selected.

2   Drag the Kids keyword tag to either one of the selected kid thumbnails. When you release the pointer, the keyword tag is applied to all selected pictures.

3   Keeping the same images selected, drag the Nature keyword tag to one of the unselected images. The keyword tag is applied to just this picture. Selecting the thumbnail or deselecting the other thumbnails is not necessary.

4   Select the image with the four children at the beach—the one with the Family sub-category keyword tag applied. Then, choose Window > Properties to open the Properties palette.

💡 *You can also show or hide the Properties panel by holding down the Alt key, and then pressing the Enter key.*

5   Select the Keyword Tags tab (📑) in the Properties palette to see which keyword tags are applied to this image.

6   Remove the Family keyword tag from the image by doing one of the following:

•   Right-click the blue keyword tag image underneath the thumbnail in the Photo Browser, and then choose Remove Family sub-category Keyword Tag from the menu.

•   Right-click the thumbnail image and choose Remove Keyword Tag > Family from the context menu.

•   In the Properties palette, right-click the Family, Kids listing, and then choose Remove Family sub-category Keyword Tag from the menu.

7   Close the Properties palette by clicking the Close button (✖) in the upper right corner of the palette, or by choosing Window > Properties again.

Creating and applying new keyword tags

In the previous topic, you created new keyword tag categories and subcategories. In this topic, you'll create a new keyword tag and specify its location.

1 Under Keyword Tags in the Organize panel, click the Create New button (✚) and choose New Keyword Tag from the menu. The Create Keyword Tag dialog box appears.

2 In the Create Keyword Tag dialog box, choose Family (under People) for category and type **Lilly** for Name, and then click OK.

3 Drag the picture from the previous exercise, the four children at the beach, to the Lilly keyword tag under Keyword Tags. The image becomes the tag icon because it's the first image to get this tag. You will adjust the tag icon in the next steps, before applying the new keyword tag to additional photos.

4 Under Keyword Tags in the Organize panel, select the Lilly keyword tag, and then click the Edit button (✐) above the list of keyword tags. Or, right-click the Lilly keyword tag, and then choose Edit Lilly keyword tag from the context menu.

5 In the Edit Keyword Tag dialog box, click the Edit Icon button to open the Edit Keyword Tag Icon dialog box.

6   In the Edit Keyword Tag Icon dialog box, drag the corners of the boundary in the thumbnail so that it surrounds just the face of the girl with the flowers in the center of the photo.

7   Click OK to close the dialog box and click OK again to close the Edit Keyword Tag dialog box.

> 💡 *You can later update the keyword tag icon when you find another photo that you think works better as keyword tag icon.*

8   Drag the Lilly keyword tag to the picture of Lilly on the pony next to her mother. The Lilly keyword tag is now applied to two images.

Converting keyword tags and categories

Changing the hierarchy of categories and keyword tags, and promoting or demoting them whenever you like is easy. Doing this does not remove the keyword tags or categories from the images to which you've assigned them.

1   Click the empty Find box next to the Kids sub-category. A binoculars icon (👀) appears in the Find box to remind you that it is selected. Only the thumbnails tagged with the Kids keyword tag are displayed in the Photo Browser.

2   Click the Show All button above the Photo Browser to see all images.

3   Under the People category, right-click the Kids sub-category and choose Edit Kids sub-category from the context menu.

4 In the Edit Sub-Category dialog box, select None (Convert to Category) from the Parent Category or Sub-Category menu, and then click OK.

Now Kids is no longer a sub-category under People but a category on its own. Its icon has been inherited from its former parent category.

5 (Optional) Select a different category icon by choosing Edit Kids category.

6 Click the empty Find box next to the Kids category. Notice that the selection of images tagged with the Kids tag did not change. Click the Show All button.

7 Under Keyword Tags, drag the Kids category to the People category.

Now the Kids category appears as a sub-category under People. Because it's no longer a category, it has the generic sub-category icon.

8 Click the empty Find box next to the Kids sub-category. Notice that the selection of images tagged with the Kids tag did not change. Click the Show All button.

9 Under the Family category, right-click the Kids sub-category and choose Change Kids sub-category to a keyword tag from the context menu.

10 Under Keyword Tags, right-click the Kids keyword tag and choose Edit Kids keyword tag from the context menu. In the Edit Keyword Tag dialog box, click the Edit Icon button. In the Edit Keyword Tag Icon dialog box, select a different image for this tag by clicking on the arrows under the thumbnail image.

11 Click OK to close the Edit Keyword Tag Icon dialog box and click OK again to close the Edit Keyword Tag dialog box.

Applying more keyword tags to images

There are a few simple ways to automatically tag multiple images, as well as manual methods you can use for applying custom tags.

1   Click the Display button (■) near the upper right corner of the Organizer window, and then choose Folder Location from the menu.

2   Click the Instant Keyword Tag icon on the right end of the separator bar above the thumbnails of BATCH1. That way you can quickly apply the same keyword tag to all items in that group.

3   In the Create and Apply New Keyword Tag dialog box, choose Other in the Category menu, leaving BATCH1 for Name, and then click OK.

4   Repeat Steps 2 and 3 for the other folder groups, BATCH2 and BATCH3.

5   Switch back to Thumbnail View, using the same menu you used in Step 1.

6   Click and drag to apply the Nature keyword tag to any image you'd like to see in that category.

7 (Optional) Create and apply any other keyword tags or categories you might want. For example, you could create a keyword tag in the Places category, naming it after the location where the pictures have been taken.

Creating a keyword tag for working files

You can create a keyword tag to apply to the files you create and save in the Organizer, as you work through the book.

1 Open the Photoshop Elements Organizer. If Show All appears above the Browser View, click it.

2 Under Keyword Tags in the Organize panel, click the Create New button, and then choose New Category from the menu.

3 In the Create Category dialog box, type **Work Files** *as the Category name and select one of the Category icons. You can scroll to the right to see other icons. Click OK.*

4 Apply this keyword tag to all the files you create while working through the lessons in this book.

Automatically finding faces for tagging

When you use the Find Faces for Tagging command, Photoshop Elements isolates and displays faces in photos so that you can quickly tag them. This makes it easy to tag faces of friends or family members. Thumbnails of individual faces appear in the Face Tagging dialog box, where you can apply existing tags or create and apply new tags. As you apply tags to faces in the Face Tagging dialog box, Photoshop Elements removes those faces, making it easier to find and tag the remaining faces. You can select Show Already Tagged Faces if you want the faces to remain after you tag them.

1   Choose Edit > Select All to select all of the photos in the Photo Browser section of the Organizer.

2   Choose Find > Find Faces for Tagging.

Photoshop Elements processes the photos and searches for faces. Thumbnails of the faces display in the Face Tagging dialog box.

*A. Select to show faces already tagged or deselect to hide those faces. **B.** Keyword tags.*
*C. Recently used keyword tags. **D.** Full context image of the most recently selected face.*

Note: *If you press Ctrl as you choose Find > Find Faces for Tagging, Photoshop Elements will produce more accurate results (for example, it will find more faces in the background of a busy photo), but it will take longer for the faces to appear. You can select your preferred* *searching method as default under Face Tagging in the Keyword Tags and Albums section of the Preferences dialog box (Edit > Preferences > Keyword Tags and Albums).*

3 In the Face Tagging dialog box, drag the Lilly keyword tag onto a face (Lilly wears the red helmet), or drag a face onto the Lilly keyword tag. You can apply other tags in the same manner, and apply keyword tags to a selection of multiple images. Once tagged, a face disappears from the display.

4 Select the Show Already Tagged Faces option to show the already tagged faces.

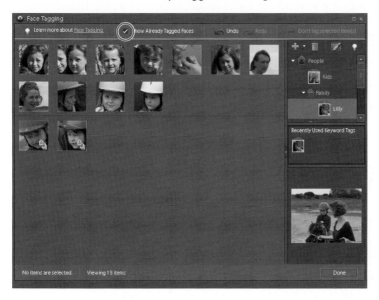

5 Click Done.

You'll use keyword tags throughout this book as a way to locate and organize lesson files.

Using keyword tags to find pictures

Why create and apply all these keyword tags? Because they make it amazingly simple to find your pictures.

1 In the Organizer, click the empty Find box next to the Kids keyword tag. A binoculars icon appears in the Find box to remind you that it is selected. Only the thumbnails tagged with the Kids keyword tag are displayed. *(See illustration on next page.)*

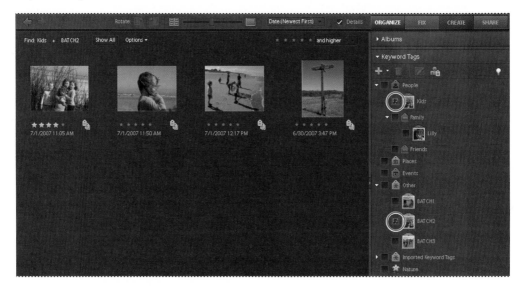

2   Leave the Kids keyword tag selected. Click the Find box for the BATCH2 keyword tag. Only four thumbnails appear: those tagged with both the Kids and the BATCH2 keyword tags.

3   From the Options menu above the Photo Browser, select Show close match results. The thumbnails display changes, also showing images that are tagged with some but not all of the selected keyword tags. These *close matches* are identified by a check mark in the upper left corner of the thumbnail images.

4   Click Show All to display all images.

Congratulations! You've finished the lesson, and we're hoping that you feel pretty good about your accomplishment.

In this lesson, you've imported files into the Organizer using various techniques and you've used several ways to view your Organizer catalog. You've also created, edited, and applied keyword tags to individual photographs so that they'll be easy to find in future work sessions.

Review

▶ Review questions

1   How do you open the Organizer component of Adobe Photoshop Elements?

2   Name three methods to import photos located on your computer hard disk into your Organizer catalog.

3   What are "watched folders"?

4   Explain the difference between Photo Brower view and Date view in the Organizer.

▶ Review answers

1   There are several ways to open the Organizer. Click Organize in the row of shortcut buttons across the lower part of the Welcome Screen when you start Photoshop Elements. Or, if the Photoshop Elements Editor is already open, click the Organizer button located to the right in the menu bar. If you always want to open Photoshop Elements in the Organizer, use the Start Up In menu in the lower left corner of the Welcome Screen to choose the Organizer.

2   This lesson demonstrated three different methods to import the three batches of photos into the Organizer:

• Use the drag-and-drop technique to add photographs from a Windows Explorer window into the Organizer catalog.

• Choose File > Get Photos and Videos > From Files and Folders, and then navigate to the folder containing your photos. You can select those images you want to add to your catalog.

• Choose File > Get Photos and Videos > By Searching, and then select the folder on the hard disk containing your photos for Look In. This method can collect all images in that folder and its subfolders.

3   Watched folders are folders on your computer that automatically alert Photoshop Elements when a new photo is saved or added to the folder. By default, the My Pictures folder is watched, and you can add additional folders to the list. New images added to these folders can be automatically added to the Organizer.

4 The default Photo Browser view of the Organizer lets you browse thumbnail images of your photos sorted by chronologic order, folder location, or import batches. In Date view you can quickly find photos taken on a particular day, month, or year.

3 | Advanced Organizing

Working with hundreds or thousands of images can be a daunting task. But rest assured, Photoshop Elements 6.0 comes to the rescue with advanced organizing options that not only get the job done but in fact make the work quite enjoyable.

In this lesson, you will learn how to do the following:

- Use advanced import options in the Photo Downloader.
- Acquire still frames from a video.
- Import pictures from a PDF document.
- Import pictures from a scanner.
- Use Version sets and Stacks to organize photos.
- Place and find photos by location using a Yahoo Map.
- Utilize other methods to find photos.
- Create Albums and Smart Albums.

Before you begin, make sure that you have correctly copied the Lessons folder from the CD in the back of this book onto your computer's hard disk. See "Copying the Classroom in a Book files" on page 3.

Getting started

In this lesson, you're going to work primarily in the Organizer component of Photoshop Elements. You will only briefly switch to the Full Edit component to import photos from a video and a PDF document. You'll also create a new catalog to manage the image files for this lesson.

1 Start Photoshop Elements, either by double-clicking the shortcut on your desktop or by choosing Start > Programs > Adobe Photoshop Elements 6.0.

2 Do one of the following:

• If the Welcome Screen appears, click Organize in the row of shortcut buttons across the lower part of the Welcome Screen.

• If Photoshop Elements 6.0 (Editor) opens without first displaying the Welcome Screen, click the Welcome Screen button (⌂) located to the left in the menu bar to display the Welcome Screen, and then click Organize. Or, click the Organizer button (⊞) located to the right in the menu bar. Then, wait until the Organizer has finished opening.

• If Photoshop Elements 6.0 (Organizer) opens, continue with step 3.

3 In the Organizer, choose File > Catalog.

4 In the Catalog Manager dialog box, click New.

5 In the Enter a name for the new catalog dialog box, type **Lesson3** as file name, deselect the Import free music into this catalog option, and then click OK.

Now you have a special catalog that you'll use just for this lesson. All you need is some pictures to put in it.

Advanced Import Options

In Lesson 2 you've learned how to import photos into the Organizer and how then to apply tags to organize them. Here you will find out how some options already available during the import process can make organizing your pictures even easier. You will also learn how to import photos from other sources, namely capturing a frame from a movie, extracting images embedded in a PDF document, and acquiring an image from a scanner.

Photo Downloader options

If you have an available digital camera or memory card from your camera with pictures on it, you can step through this exercise using your own pictures. For best results, you should have several batches of pictures taken at different times on a single day. Alternatively, you can simply follow the process by studying the illustrations provided, without actually performing the exercise yourself.

1   Connect your digital camera or the card reader for your digital camera to your computer, following the manufacturer's instructions for your camera.

2   Do the following:

• If the Windows Auto Play dialog box appears, click Cancel.

• If the Photo Downloader dialog box appears automatically, continue with step 3.

• If the Photo Downloader dialog box does not appear automatically, choose File > Get Photos and Videos > From Camera or Card Reader.

3   If the Photo Downloader dialog box opens in the Advanced mode, click the Standard Dialog button located near the lower left corner of the dialog box. Under Source in the standard mode Photo Downloader dialog box, choose from the Get Photos from menu the name of the connected camera or card reader.

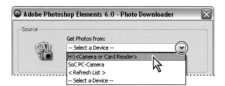

4   Under Import Settings, accept the folder location listed next to Location, or click Browse to choose a new location for the files.

5   Without making any other changes to the settings, click the Advanced Dialog button in the lower left corner of the dialog box.

Thumbnail images of all photos on your camera or card reader appear in the Advanced dialog box. You also have access to several options not available in the Standard dialog box.

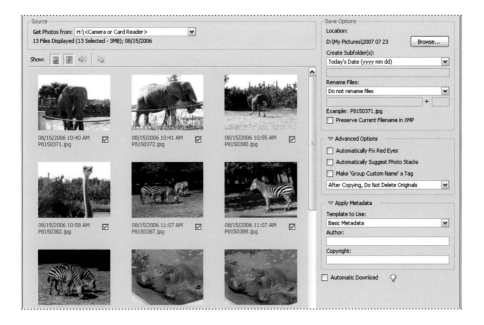

6 Under Save Options, choose Custom Groups (Advanced) from the Create Subfolder(s) menu. Your selection is reflected in the pathname displayed next to Location.

The thumbnail images on the left side of the dialog box are divided into groups, based on the time and date the photos were taken.

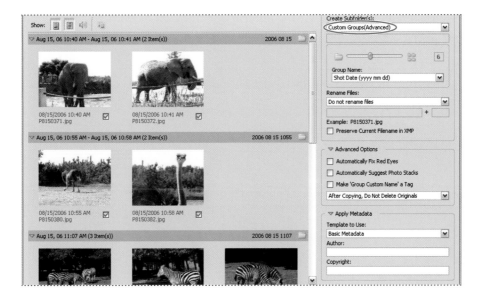

7 Use the slider under the Create Subfolder(s) menu to adjust the granularity of the subdivision to suit your needs. Move the slider to the left to generate fewer groups (or subfolders), or move the slider to the right to generate more groups. Scroll down the list of thumbnail images to review the grouping of the images. The number of groups chosen is displayed in the box to the right of the slider.

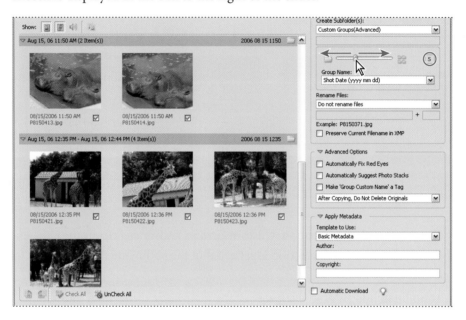

You can increase or decrease the number of groups one by one by typing Control-Shift-M or Control-Shift-L respectively on your keyboard.

8 Choose Shot Date (yyyy mm dd) + Custom Name from the Group Name menu.

9 On the right end of the separator bar above the thumbnails of the first group, click the Custom Name field and type **Elephant** into the text box that appears.

10 Repeat step 9 for all other groups in the thumbnail list, giving each group a distinct name (in this example, that could be **Ostrich**, **Zebra**, **Hippo**, and **Giraffe**).

11 Under Advanced Options, select the Make 'Group Custom Name' a Tag check box. This will automatically create appropriate tags and apply them to the pictures when imported in the Organizer. If they are selected, deselect the check boxes for Automatically Fix Red Eyes and the Automatically Suggest Photo Stacks.

12 Click Get Photos.

The photos are copied from the camera to the specified group folder locations.

13 If the Files Successfully Copied dialog box appears, click OK.

The Getting Photos dialog box appears and the photos are imported into Photoshop Elements. The tags for the groups are created and applied, and the imported photos appear in the Photo Browser.

Other options available in the Advanced Photo Download dialog box include picking and choosing which files to import, rotating images, applying red eye fix, suggesting photo stacks, and adding metadata like name and copyright information. The more of these options you can take advantage of when importing files into the Organizer, the less work you will have later on to manage and organize your files, and the easier it will be to find a specific photo again months or even years after it has been imported. Later in this lesson, you'll hear more about organizing your photos. But first, you'll learn about other options to import images into your catalog.

Acquiring still frames from a video

You can capture frames from your digital videos if they are saved in a file format that Photoshop Elements can open, including AVI, MPG, MPEG, WMV, ASF, and MLV. To capture frames from video, you'll need to open the Editor.

1   If you have any image selected in the Organizer from the previous exercise, choose Edit > Deselect.

2   Click the Editor button (⬚) located near the top right corner of the Organizer window, and then choose Full Edit from the menu. Wait until the Editor has finished opening.

3   In the Editor, choose File > Import > Frame From Video.

4   In the Frame From Video dialog box, click the Browse button. In the Open dialog box, navigate to the Lesson03 folder and select the file Video.avi, and then click Open.

5   To start the video, click the Play button (▶). Click the Pause button (⏸) after about 4 seconds, and then use the arrow keys on your keyboard to move forward or backward one frame at a time until you find a frame you would like to capture.

Note: Some video formats don't support rewinding or fast-forwarding. In these cases, the Rewind (◄◄) and Fast Forward (►►) buttons are dimmed.

6   To get a frame of the video as a still image, click the Grab Frame button or press the spacebar when the frame is visible on the screen.

7   (Optional) You can move forward and backward in the video to capture additional frames.

8   When you have all the frames you want, click Done.

Depending on your video footage, you might notice artifacts in the still image resulting from the fact that a video picture consists of two interlaced half-pictures. The odd-numbered scanlines of the image, also called odd fields, constitute one half-picture, and the even-numbered scanlines, the even fields, the other. Since the two half-pictures of the video were recorded at slightly different times, the captured still image might look distorted.

You can remedy this problem by using Photoshop Elements' De-Interlace filter. With the De-Interlace filter you can remove either the odd or even fields in a video image and replace the discarded lines by duplication or interpolation from the remaining lines.

9   With the captured still image selected in the Editor, choose Filter > Video > De-Interlace. In the De-Interlace dialog box, choose either Odd Fields or Even Fields under Eliminate and either Duplication or Interpolation under Create New Fields by, and

then click OK. Which combination of options to choose for best results depends on the actual image at hand.

A still frame picture captured from video footage, before and after the De-Interlace filter has been applied (image detail at 300% magnification).

10 Save your work in the My CIB Work folder, and then close the image window in the Editor.

Importing from a PDF document

Photoshop Elements enables you to import whole pages or just selected images from a PDF document.

1 In the Editor, choose File > Open.

2 In the Open dialog box, navigate to the Lesson03 folder and select the file PDF_File.pdf, and then click Open.

Note: If you can't see the file PDF_File.pdf, make sure you have either All Formats or Photoshop PDF (*.PDF, *.PDP) selected in the Files of type menu.

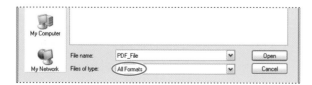

In the Import PDF dialog box, you can choose to import entire pages, or just the images from the PDF file. If your PDF file contains multiple pages, you can control-click the page thumbnail images to select just the pages you want to import. Likewise, you can selectively import one or more images from the PDF file. Pages are rasterized according to your choice of images size, resolution, and color mode. The result will be an image of each page, similar to an image acquired by scanning in a document.

3   Under Select in the Import PDF dialog box, choose Images.

4   Select Fit Page from the Thumbnail Size menu to see the preview images as large as possible. Use the scrollbar on the right to scroll down to the last image.

5   Click to select the image you want to import. Optionally, control-click any additional images you want to import at the same time. Then, click OK.

Each selected image opens in its own document window in the Editor, ready for further processing.

6   For each imported image choose File > Save As, navigate to the My CIB Work folder, and save the file with a descriptive name in Photoshop (*.PSD,*.PDD) file format. Select the Include in the Organizer option before you click Save, if you want to add the files to your catalog.

Scanning images

This exercise is optional and requires that you have an available scanner.

Note: Photoshop Elements 6.0 allows you to scan images using a video input source like a web camera attached to your computer.

1   To prepare for acquiring images from a scanner, choose Edit > Preferences > Scanner, and then do the following:

• If you have more than one scanner or an additional video input source installed, make sure that the correct scanner is selected in the Scanner menu.

• Either leave unchanged the default settings for Save As (jpeg), and Quality (6 Medium), or if you want different settings, change them now.

• Deselect the Automatically Fix Red Eyes check box. You will learn in Lesson 8, "Repairing and Retouching Images," how to fix red eye in the Organizer.

• If you want to change the location to which the scanned files will be saved, click Browse. Then, find and select the folder you want to use.

• Click OK to close the Preferences dialog box.

2   Place the picture or document you want to scan in the scanner bed and make sure your scanner is turned on.

3   If the scan dialog box does not appear automatically, go to the Organizer and choose File > Get Photos and Videos > From Scanner.

4   In the scan dialog box, click the Preview button and examine the resulting image.

Note: The general appearance of the dialog box and the options available for your scanner may vary from those shown in the illustrations.

5   (Optional) If you want to make adjustments, change the settings as preferred.

6   Click Scan.

When the scan is complete, the image thumbnail appears in the Organizer.

7   Click Back to All Images to see your entire catalog.

When you scan several photographs together, Photoshop Elements can automatically crop the scan into individual photos and straighten them. For more information on the Divide Scanned Photos feature, see Photoshop Elements Help.

Organizing photos

Organizing files and folders efficiently can be challenging. It's easy to forget which pictures are stored in what folder, and having to open and examine the content of numerous folders to look for files or images can be time consuming and tedious.

With the Organizer, such searches are now a thing of the past. The next set of topics will show you how investing a little time in organizing your pictures can streamline the process of sorting through your image files, regardless of where they are stored.

Working with Version sets

A version set groups one original photo and edited versions of the original. Version sets make it easy to find both the edited versions of an image and the original, because they are visually stacked together instead of scattered throughout the Photo Browser.

Now you'll use Auto Smart Fix to edit an image in the organizer and create a version set. To start off, you'll clear all the images you might have added to the catalog since the beginning of this lesson.

1   With the Lesson3.psa catalog open in the Organizer, if you see the Show All button above the Photo Browser, click it. Choose Edit > Select All, and then choose Edit > Delete from Catalog. If available in the Confirm Deletion from Catalog dialog box, select the Delete all photos in collapsed stacks and the Delete all items in collapsed version sets option, and then click OK.

2   Choose File > Get Photos and Videos > From Files and Folders.

3   In the Get Photos from Files and Folders dialog box, navigate to the Lesson03 folder and select the Photos folder. Select the Get Photos From Subfolders check box. If selected, deselect the Automatically Fix Red Eyes and the Automatically Suggest Photo Stacks check boxes, and then click Get Photos.

4   In the Import Attached Tags dialog box, click Select All, and then click OK. Click OK to close any other alert dialog box. Click the Show All button above the Photo Browser.

You can now see the thumbnails of the images you added to your Lesson 3 catalog in the Photo Browser.

5   Under Keyword Tags, click the triangle next to Imported Keyword Tags to see the newly added keyword tags.

6   In the Photo Browser, select the first photo of the Elephant, taken at 10:40 am, and then choose Edit > Auto Smart Fix. The Auto Smart Fix command corrects the overall color balance and improves shadow and highlight detail, if necessary. The edited copy of the photo is automatically grouped with the original photo in a version set.

Version sets are identified by a version set icon in the upper right corner of an image.

Note: *If you edit a photo in the Organizer, a version set is automatically created for you. If you edit the photo in the Editor and choose File > Save As, you can select the Save in Version Set with Original option to put the photo and its edited copy together in a version set.*

7   Click the expand button on the right side of the thumbnail image, to see the original and edited images in a version set.

8   To see only the topmost photo in a version set, click the collapse button on the right side of the last thumbnail image in the version set, or right-click any of the thumbnail images in the expanded view of the version set, and then choose Version Set > Collapse Items in Version Set from the context menu. Notice the other commands available from the same context menu—as well as from the Edit menu—such as converting all images in a version set into individual photos in the catalog (Version Set > Convert Version Set to Individual Items).

Note: *If you edit a photo that's already in a version set, the edited copy is placed at the top of the existing version set. To specify a different photo as the topmost, select it in the expanded view of the version set, and then choose Edit > Version Set > Set as Top Item.*

About stacks

You can create stacks to visually group a set of similar photos together, making them easy to manage. Stacks are useful for keeping multiple photos of the same subject in one place, and they reduce clutter in the Photo Browser.

For instance, you can create a stack to group together multiple photos of your family taken with the same pose, or for photos taken at a sports event using your camera's burst mode or auto-bracket feature. Generally, when you take photos this way, you end up with many variations of the same photo, but you only want the best one to appear in the Photo Browser. Stacking the photos lets you easily access them all in one place instead of having them scattered across rows of thumbnails.

1   Click the empty Find box next to the Zebra tag in the Imported Tags category.

2   To marquee-select all images, click below the first thumbnail image and drag to the top and right. When you release the pointer, all images within the selection box are selected.

3   Choose Edit > Stack > Stack Selected Photos.

All the Zebra photos are now grouped in a stack. You can expand and collapse stacks in the Photo Browser the same way you expand and collapse version sets.

*Stacks are identified by a stack icon
in the upper right corner of an image.*

4   Click the Show All button above the Photo Browser, and then click the empty Find
boxes next to the Hippo and the Ostrich tags in the Imported Tags category.

5   Choose Edit > Select All, and then choose Edit > Stack > Automatically Suggest
Photo Stacks.

The Automatically Suggest Photo Stacks dialog box appears. The two photos of the
hippopotamus have been successfully placed in a group already, but the ostrich photos
will need to be grouped manually.

6　In the Automatically Suggest Photo Stacks dialog box, scroll down to the bottom of the thumbnail list. Click the photo of the ostrich in the last group and drag it up to place it in one group with the other ostrich photo.

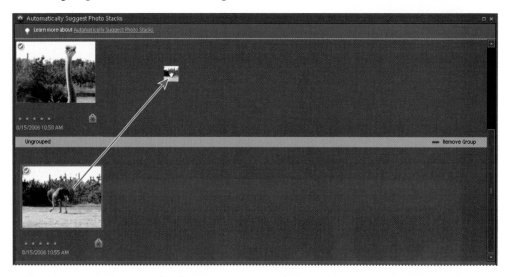

7　To split one group into two, position the cursor between two images of the first group and when the cursor changes to the scissors icon, click to split the group.

8　To exclude all photos in a group from being stacked, click the Remove Group button. Or, select individual photos, and then click the Remove Selected Photo(s) button in the lower left corner of the dialog box.

9   If you change your mind about photos excluded from being stacked, make sure the Show Removed Photos check box at the bottom of the dialog box is selected. Then, drag the thumbnail image from the removed photos bin to add it to a group in the main thumbnail area.

10   When done, click Stack All Groups to close the Automatically Suggest Photo Stacks dialog box and to stack the photos in each group. Click Show All in the Photo Browser.

Stacks are identified by a stack icon in the upper right corner of an image.

Note: *If you edit a photo that's already in a stack, the photo and its edited copy are put in a version set that is nested in the original stack.*

Tips for working with stacks

Keep these points in mind when working with stacks:

• By default, the newest photo is placed on top of the stack. As you create the stack, you can specify a new top photo by right-clicking that photo and using the context menus.

• Combining two or more stacks merges them to form one new stack. The original stacks are not preserved. The newest photo is placed on top of the stack.

• Many actions applied to a stack, such as editing, e-mailing, and printing, are applied to the topmost item only. To apply an action to all photos in a stack, reveal the stacked photos or unstack the photos.

• If you apply a keyword tag to a collapsed stack, the keyword tag is applied to all items in the stack. When you run a search on the keyword tag, the top photo with the stack icon appears in the search results. If you want to apply a keyword tag to only one photo in a stack, reveal that photo in the stack, and then apply the keyword tag.

• You can access stack commands by right-clicking or by using the Edit menu.

Creating Albums

Another way of grouping photos is to organize them in albums. Think of a Photoshop Elements Album as being the equivalent of a physical photo album. You can, for example, create a new album for a special occasion like a wedding, or to collect images you want to use in a project such as a slideshow. Then, you add pictures to the album the same way you would associate pictures with keyword tags. The main difference between albums and keyword tags is that in albums you can arrange the photos into any order you want. Smart albums are a special sort of album. They contain photos matching a search criteria rather than being manually assembled. You'll learn more about smart albums later in this lesson under "Viewing and finding photos."

1   If necessary, click the triangle next to Albums in the Organize bin to expand the palette.

2   To create a new album, click the Create New button (✚) under Albums in the Organize bin, and then choose New Album from the menu.

3   In the Create Album dialog box, type **Animals** for Name, and then click OK.

4   Ctrl-click to select two or three photos in the Photo Browser, and then drag the group onto the Animals album icon.

Note: If you add a collapsed version set or a collapsed stack to an album, only the topmost picture of the version set or stack will be visible in the album. To add a different picture to the album, first expand the version set or stack.

5 To see the content of an album, click the album icon, or drag and drop the album icon onto the Find bar above the Photo Browser. Notice the number in the top left corner of each photo, representing its order in the album.

Note: You can only view one album at a time.

6 To change the order in an album, select one or more photos in the Photo Browser, and then drag the selection to its new position. The photos are reordered when you release the pointer.

7 (Optional) To remove a picture from an album, right-click the picture in the album view, and then choose Remove from Album > *[album name]* from the menu.

8 Click Show All above the Browser View to see all photos in your catalog.

💡 *You can group related albums in an album group—similar to grouping keyword tags in categories. You can change an album's properties and icon by clicking the Edit album button—similar to using the Edit keyword tag button for keyword tags.*

9 To delete an album, right-click its icon in the Albums palette, and then choose Delete *[album name]* album from the menu.

10 Click OK in the Confirm Album Deletion dialog box.

Note: Deleting an album does not delete any photos from your catalog. Albums store only references to the actual photos.

The Map View

In the Map view of the Organizer, you can arrange photos by geographic location. You can drag photos from the Photo Browser directly to a location on the map. In the Map view, you can then search for and view photos in specific geographic locations.

1 In the Organizer, right-click the thumbnail image of the elephant, and then choose Place on Map from the context menu.

2 In the Photo Location on Map dialog box, type **1 Zoo Road, San Francisco, CA** in the text box, and then click Find.

Note: You must have an active Internet connection to use this feature.

3 In the Look Up Address dialog box, click OK to confirm 1 Zoo Rd San Francisco, CA, 94132-1027 US.

4 In the Map view that opens to the left of the Browser view you can use the Hand tool to drag the map in any direction. The red pin indicates the location for your photo.

5 Select Hybrid from the menu in the bottom right corner of the Map view.

6 Use the Zoom In tool and the Hand tool in combination to magnify the view on the San Francisco Zoological Gardens. Use the Move tool to reposition the red pin to exactly where you want it to appear on the map. *(See illustration on next page.)*

7   To place additional photos on the map, drag them from the Photo Browser to the Map view. If you get too close to an existing pin, the photos will be grouped under one pin location—this may or may not be what you want.

You can drag a keyword tag (e.g. a keyword tag in the Places category) to the Map view to position all photos tagged with this keyword tag on the map.

8 Select the Limit Search to Map Area check box in the lower left corner of the Map View. Only photos mapped to the currently visible map area are displayed in the Browser View.

9 To hide the Map view, click the Close button (✖) in the upper right corner of the Map View. Click the Show All button above the Photo Browser. Right-click the thumbnail image of the first elephant, and then choose Show on Map from the context menu. The Map view will open, displaying the location to which the photo was mapped.

10 Hide the Map view.

This concludes the section on organizing your photos. You've learned about version sets and stacks, how to group photos in albums, and how to arrange photos by their geographic location using the Map view. In the next section, you will learn how you can find photos in your catalog even if not much time was spent on properly organizing them.

Viewing and finding photos

In the Organizer, Photoshop Elements lets you find photos using several methods:

- **Timeline**—If necessary, choose Window > Timeline to display the timeline above the Browser View. Then, click a month or set a range to find photos and media files chronologically by date, or by import batch or folder location.

- **Find bar**—Drag and drop a photo, keyword tag, creation, or album onto the find bar to locate matching or similar photos and media files.

- **Find menu**—Use the commands in this menu to find photos by date, caption or note, file name, history, media type, metadata, or color similarity. Commands are also available for finding photos and media files that have unknown dates, are untagged, or are not in any album.

Finding photos by visual similarity

You can search for photos containing similar images, color, or general appearance.

1   In the Organizer, choose Edit > Select All. Choose Edit > Stack > Unstack Photos, and then choose Edit > Version Set > Revert to Original. Click OK to close any alert dialog box that might appear.

2   Choose Edit > Deselect. Then, drag the first image with the zebras to the find bar.

Photos are displayed in decreasing order of similarity in visual appearance. A similarity percentage appears in the bottom left corner of each image.

3   Click the Show All button.

Finding photos using details and metadata

You can search for your images by file details or metadata. Searching by metadata is useful when you want to search using multiple criteria at once. For example, if you want to find all photos captured on a certain date that are marked with a specific keyword tag, you can search using both capture date and keyword tags in the Find by Details (Metadata) dialog box.

Searchable metadata includes file name, file type, keyword tags, albums, notes, author, map location, and capture date, as well as camera model, shutter speed, and F-stop—to name just a few of the many available search criteria.

Here you will search for photos taken near a specific location using the Find by Details (Metadata) dialog box.

1   Choose Find > By Details (Metadata) in the Organizer to display the Find by Details (Metadata) dialog box.

2   Under Search Criteria, click the first menu, and then use the scrollbar to scroll down towards the end of the list. While scrolling, notice the many options available as search criteria. Some meta data is generated automatically for each picture, some is added and available only when you spend time organizing your catalog. For this exercise, choose the last entry in the list, Map Location.

3   From the menu next to Map Location, choose Within.

4   Click the magnifying glass button to open the Photo location on Map dialog box. In the Photo location on Map dialog box, enter **1 Zoo Road, San Francisco, CA** as address, and then click Find. Click OK to close the Photo location on Map dialog box.

5   In the Find by Details (Metadata) dialog box, enter **1** as distance and choose Miles from the last menu.

Note: To include other metadata values in your search, click the plus (+) sign and specify new values using the menus that appear. To remove metadata from your search, click the minus (-) sign along the right side of the metadata you want to remove. If you specify more than one search criteria, click the appropriate radio button to search for files matching any or all of the search criteria.

6 If selected, deselect the Save this Search Criteria as Smart Album check box. You'll learn about smart albums in the last part of this lesson. Then, click the Search button. All images that match the specified criteria are displayed.

7 (Optional) To modify the search, click Options in the find bar, and then choose Modify Search Criteria from the menu. This will open the Find by Details (Metadata) dialog box with the current search criteria entered. Make your changes, and then click Search to display your new results in the Photo Browser.

8 Click the Show All button in the find bar.

Viewing and managing files by folder location

The Folder Location view in the Organizer splits the Photo Browser into three sections: a folder hierarchy panel on the left, an image thumbnail panel in the center, and the Palette Bin on the right. From this view you can manage your folders, add files to your catalog, automatically tag files using their folder name as the keyword tag, and add or remove folders from Watched Folder status.

By default, the left panel displays all the folders on your hard disk, and the center panel displays only the thumbnails of the managed files in the selected folder. Folders containing managed files have a Managed folder icon (▣). Watched folders have a Watched folder icon (▣).

1 Click the Display button (⬛) near the upper right corner of the Organizer window, and then choose Folder Location from the menu.

The folder hierarchy appears on the left side of the Photo Browser and the image thumbnails appear in the center.

The contents of a selected folder are displayed when using Folder Location view.

Note: *You can change the default view for each panel by choosing Edit > Preferences > Folder Location View and selecting the options you want.*

2 Do one of the following to specify which files appear in the center panel:

• To view only the managed files in the selected folder, right-click in the left panel and deselect Show All Files.

- To view all your managed files in the center panel grouped by folder location, right-click in the left panel and select Show All Files.

- If you want to search all your managed files while in Folder Location view, select Show All Files.

- To find the folder location of a file, click the file's thumbnail in the center panel. The file's folder is highlighted in the left panel.

- To find files in a specific folder, click the folder in the left panel. Thumbnails for the files in that folder appear in the center panel, grouped under the folder name.

- To instantly tag files by their folder locations, click the Instant Keyword Tag icon in the center panel on the right side of the window. In the Create and Apply New Keyword Tag dialog box you can attach keyword tags simultaneously to all images in that folder.

3 To manage files and folders, select a folder and do any of the following:

- To move a file to a different folder, drag the file's thumbnail from the center panel to a folder in the left panel.

- To view the folder in Windows Explorer, right-click in the left panel and choose Reveal in Explorer.

- To add or remove the folder from watched-folder status, right-click in the left panel and choose Add to Watched Folders or Remove from Watched Folders.

- To add a file in the folder to your catalog, right-click in the left panel and choose Add Unmanaged Files to Catalog.

- To rename the folder, right-click in the left panel and choose Rename Folder. Then, type a new name.

- To delete the folder, right-click in the left panel and choose Delete Folder.

4 Click the Display button (■), and then choose Thumbnail View from the menu.

Working with smart albums

Smart albums, like albums, contain photos of your choosing. However, instead of manually selecting individual photos as for albums, you only need to specify search criteria to create a smart album. Once you set the criteria for a smart album, any photo in a catalog that matches the criteria will appear automatically in that smart album. As you add new photos to the catalog, those photos matching smart album criteria will appear automatically in that smart album. Smart Albums keep themselves up-to-date.

1   To set up search criteria for a new smart album, choose Find > Find by Details (Metadata). In the Find by Details (Metadata) dialog box, select the search criteria for the smart album. Click the plus sign (+) to add a criterion, click the minus sign (-) to remove a criterion.

2   If necessary, select the Save this Search Criteria as Smart Album. Enter **My first smart album** as name, and then click Search.

3   To display the photos in a smart album in the Photo Browser, select the smart album from the Albums palette.

Note: You cannot change the order of photos in a smart album, as you can for an album. Nor can you add photos to a smart album by dragging them onto the album's icon; you need to modify the album's search criteria to change the content of a smart album. The content of a smart album may change over time even without modifying the search criteria if photos matching the search criteria are added or removed from the catalog; e.g. a smart album may contain photos captured within the last six months from today's date.

4   To change the name of a smart album, do the following:

• Select the smart album from the Albums palette.

• Click the Edit button (⬛) in the Albums palette.

• Enter a new name in the Edit Smart Album dialog box, and then click OK.

5   To change the search criteria of a smart album, do the following:

• Select the smart album from the Albums palette.

• Click Options in the find bar, and then choose Modify Search Criteria from the menu.

6   Modify the search criteria in the Find by Details (Metadata) dialog box, and select to save it as smart album. Provide a new name for the smart album, and then click Search.

Note: You can save the modified search criteria using the same name, but this is not recommended. A second smart album with the same name will be created, rather than the first smart album being overwritten. A dialog box will alert you about the duplicate file name. Click OK if you want to create a second smart album with the same name anyway.

7   To delete the smart album, right-click its icon in the Albums palette, and then choose Delete *[smart album name]* album from the menu. Click OK to confirm.

Congratulations! You've reached the end of Lesson 3. In this lesson, you've learned about advanced import options in the Photo Downloader, how to acquire still frames from a video, and how to import images from a PDF file or by using a scanner. You've organized images in version sets, stacks and albums, placed photos on a map, and learned some advanced methods to find and manage photos in your catalog.

You can review and test your command of the concepts and techniques presented in this lesson by working through the following questions and answers.

Review

▶ **Review questions**

1   How can you automatically create and apply tags to images while importing them from a digital camera or card reader?

2   What does the Photoshop Elements De-Interlace filter do?

3   What does the Auto Smart Fix command do?

4   What are Version Sets and Stacks?

5   What is the main difference between grouping pictures using tags and grouping them in an album?

▶ **Review answers**

1   In the Advanced Photo Downloader dialog box, select Custom Groups (Advanced) from the Create Subfolder(s) menu. Next, select an option including Custom Name from the Group Name menu. Enter a Group Name in the Custom Name field of the separator bar in thumbnail view. Finally, select the Make 'Group Name' as a Tag check box before clicking Get Photos.

2   The Photoshop Elements De-Interlace filter can improve the appearance of still frame images acquired from a video. Depending on your video footage, you might notice artifacts in the still image, caused by the fact that a video picture consists of two interlaced half-pictures. With the De-Interlace filter you can remove either the odd or even fields in a video image and replace the discarded lines by duplication or interpolation from the remaining lines.

3   The Auto Smart Fix command corrects the overall color balance and improves shadow and highlight detail, if necessary. When invoked from within the Organizer, the Auto Smart Fix command groups the edited copy of the photo automatically with the original photo in a version set.

4   A version set groups one original photo and its edited versions. Stacks are used to group a set of similar photos, like multiple photos of your family taken with the same pose, or photos taken at a sports event using your camera's burst mode or auto-bracket feature. A version set can be nested inside a stack: if you

edit a photo that's already in a stack, the photo and its edited copy are put in a version set that is nested in the original stack.

5 The main difference between albums and keyword tags is that in albums you can arrange the photos into any order you want.

4 Creating Projects

You can quickly and easily create original and interesting projects from your photos by using templates with different themes for online galleries, photo collages, greeting cards, CD/DVD labels, slide shows, flipbooks, and so on.

Such projects enable you to combine images, text, animations, music, and narration to design unique multimedia creations that are fun to produce. Whether it's sharing your photos online, presenting a slide show, personalizing a CD or DVD label, designing a very special greeting card for your family or friends, or even printing your own coffee table book. Adobe Photoshop Elements enables you to unleash your creativity. This lesson concentrates on the design of creations, while in Lesson 5 you will learn different ways to share them.

In this lesson, you'll do the following:

- Create a greeting card.

- Present your photos in an Online gallery.

- Animate your photos in a Slideshow.

Before you begin, make sure that you have correctly copied the Lessons folder from the CD in the back of this book onto your computer's hard disk. See "Copying the Classroom in a Book files" on page 3.

Getting started

While working on the projects in this lesson, you'll use the CIB Catalog you created in the "Getting Started" section at the beginning of this book. To use the CIB Catalog, follow these steps:

1   Start Photoshop Elements, and in the Welcome Screen, click the Organize button. Then, wait until the Organizer has finished opening.

2   Choose File > Catalog.

3   In the Catalog Manager dialog box, select the CIB Catalog under Catalogs, and then click Open.

If you do not see the CIB Catalog file, review the procedures found in "Getting Started." See "Copying the Lessons files from the CD" on page 3, and "Creating a catalog" on page 4.

Creating a Greeting Card

Eye-catching greeting cards are a sure way to impress family and friends, and a really attractive card can spend many months on someone's mantelpiece, or even get framed and displayed with pride.

The Greeting Card Editor in Adobe Photoshop Elements offers you a variety of templates to create attractive cards with ease and efficiency. You can include one or more photos on each page of a greeting card that can be printed on your home printer, ordered online, or sent via e-mail.

This lesson will enable you to experience how easy it is to choose a format and theme and present a photo in a creative and professional looking manner. When you're finished, you'll have transformed your photo into a delightful greeting card.

1   In the Organizer, use the Keyword Tags palette to find the portrait of a little girl, tagged with Lesson 4, named 4_Pauline.jpg.

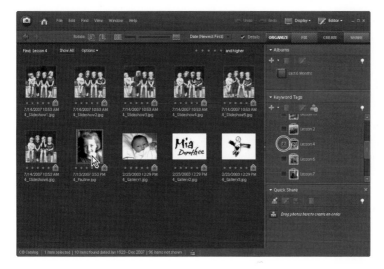

2   Click to select the purple Create tab in the Task pane.

3   In the Create panel of the Task pane, choose Greeting Card from the More Options menu.

4   In the New Greeting Card dialog box, under Choose a Theme, scroll down and select Wedding Classic, the third theme from last, showing grey torn paper with white flowers along the bottom. Under Choose a Layout, select the middle layout in the second row, a portrait format rectangle on an angle. Select the Auto-Fill with Project Bin Photos option and deselect Include Captions. Then, click Done.

5   You'll see a preview of your greeting card in the Editor panel, with a bounding box around the photo you have chosen. You can move, rotate and resize the photo if you wish. To resize the picture, position the pointer over a handle in the corner of the bounding box—the pointer turns into a double arrow—and drag to change the size. When dragging the bounding box, the image is scaled proportionally by default. Click and drag the photo if you want to reposition it on the greeting card.

6   When done resizing and repositioning the photo, click the green Commit button
(✔) at the bottom of the bounding box to commit the changes.

That was quick! Composing your photo with an appropriate theme and layout can make
a really distinctive card.

💡 *When the Move tool is selected, you can use the arrow keys on your keyboard to move the elements of a selected layer in small increments instead of dragging them using your pointer. Similarly, you can use the arrow keys to move a selection when a selection tool is active.*

7   Choose File > Save. In the Save As dialog box, navigate to the My CIB Work folder and name the file **4_Greeting_Card.psd**. Make sure that the Include in the Organizer option is selected. Click Save.

8   Choose File > Close. Be certain not to save any changes to the original photo.

Congratulations, you've finished your first creation. Now you've experienced how quickly you can get attractive results using pre-designed styles. Look for yourself, there is an abundance of styles and templates to choose from to best suit your creative projects. In Lesson 5 you will learn more about printing, sharing and exporting from the Organizer.

Working with multiple pages

Photoshop Elements enables you to create multi-page layouts. This comes in handy for any multi-page Creations—photo albums for example—where you want consistency of layout from page to page. Under Edit you have the choice of adding blank pages or using the same layout. The example shown below uses the Wedding Classic theme as background, but with a different layout from that used for the greeting card.

Presenting your photos in a Photo gallery

The next project is an online presentation of your photos. Web galleries come in a variety of layouts and designs, and are optimized for viewing images on a web page. For this project you will work on an imaginary birth announcement using an animated template.

The Online Gallery wizard will guide you through the process of adding photos, applying web page layouts and background styles, writing captions, previewing in the Browser, and sharing the files. The Online Gallery wizard only lets you arrange photos, not edit them.

Using the Online Gallery Wizard

1 Switch back to the Organizer and select the last three images from the Lesson 4 folder, 4_Gallery1.jpg, 4_Gallery2.jpg, and 4_Gallery3. jpg.

2 Select the Create panel of the Task pane, and then click Online Gallery. Under Items, only the selected three images are displayed. Then, click Next.

💡 *You can arrange the order of the photo thumbnails on the left side of the wizard. To move a thumbnail, drag a thumbnail between the other thumbnails.*

3   Choose Animated from the Select a Category menu. Under Select a Template, click the first template—featuring a baby on a blue background. Then, click Next.

💡 *The design thumbnails change according to the type of gallery you choose. For example, the Interactive gallery offers different design thumbnails than the Animated or the Web galleries.*

4   A preview of the animation you are creating will be visible in the lower part of the dialog box. *(See illustration on next page.)* At the end of the animation, the first photo included in the template will be displayed. The other pictures can be seen by clicking the previous and next buttons under the picture.

5   With your first picture visible on the right, type **Finally - here she is!** in the Title text box under Customize. Then, type **We are so proud and delighted...** in the subtitle text box and your e-mail address in the E-Mail Address text box. Click the Refresh button to see your changes applied.

6   Your captions, which are now part of the animation, are featured prominently at the upper left of your photos. Click Next.

7 Type **Birth Announcement** in the Gallery Name box, and then click the Browse button next to Save To.

8 In the Browse For Folder dialog box, select the My CIB Work folder, and then click OK to close the Browse For Folder dialog box.

9 In the Create panel, click Next. Under Share this gallery to, you have the choice between Photoshop Showcase, My FTP, or CD/DVD. For now just click Done. The preview will automatically close and you will see your saved project in the Organizer window.

Previewing in Internet Explorer

1 Switch to Internet Explorer (or your favorite Web browser).

2 Choose File > Open, and then click Browse in the Open dialog box.

3   In the Windows Internet Explorer dialog box, navigate to the My CIB Work folder. Within that folder, open the Birth Announcement folder.

4   Select the index.htm file and click Open.

5   Click OK to close the Open dialog box. Internet Explorer will open and display the animated photo gallery you just created. When done playing the animation, close your Web browser window.

Note: *To be able to view the animation, you might have to install Adobe Flash Player ActiveX Control in your Web browser.*

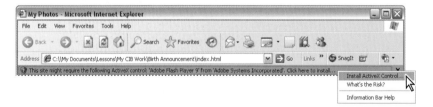

As you've just seen, with the help of the Online Gallery wizard you don't have to be a Web expert—or cause yourself a headache with a lengthy creation process—to present your images online in a professional looking manner. You will learn more about sharing your projects in Lesson 5.

Animating your photos in a slideshow

Creating slide shows is a popular feature of Photoshop Elements. It's a fun way to share your images because you can choose from an array of formats, transitions, and graphics, as well as having the option to add captions and even sound or narration.

Using the Slideshow Editor

1   Switch back to the Organizer, and select the six photos with the four girls sitting on a wall. These pictures, tagged with Lesson 4, are named 4_Slideshow1.jpg through 4_Slideshow6.jpg.

2   Select the Create panel of the Task pane, and then click the Slide Show button.

3   In the Slide Show Preference dialog box, choose 3 sec for Static Duration, Dissolve as Transition, and 2 sec for the Transition Duration. Deselect the Include Photo Captions as Text option and select Landscape Photos next to Crop to Fit Slide. You can leave the other settings unchanged. *(See illustration on next page.)* Click OK and your project will automatically open in the Slide Show Editor window.

4   Click the Play button (▶) located below the preview panel, or press the spacebar to start the slide show. Although you'll see the four girls and their changing visual expressions during the presentation of those six images, the transition from one picture to the next seems too fast and needs to be adjusted.

Add Music and Narration to a slide show

Sound adds yet another dimension to the animation of your images and complements your work. You can add an ambitious, full-scale soundtrack or simply record narration. You can import music from your Photoshop Elements catalog or from any location on your computer. In the Slide Show dialog box, click Add Media, and then navigate to the place where your music files are located.

In the Add Audio dialog box, you can listen to a clip before adding it by selecting the clip and clicking Play. To align the pace of the slide show with the music, select Fit Slides To Audio (the length of each slide is updated in the film strip). You can also drag the audio file to begin playing on a specific slide.

You can record voice narration to a slide if you have a microphone attached to your computer. You can also attach the narration to the photo as an audio caption. You'll find the narration button in the Extras palette of the Slide Show dialog box,

For more information regarding adding music and narration, please consult the Photoshop Elements Help file.

Refining the Slide Show

In the next steps, you will adjust the transitions and change the order of the images.

1   From the menu in the Slide Show Editor window, choose Edit > Select All Transitions.

2   In the Properties panel, reduce the time to 1 sec under Multiple Transitions, and select Clock Wipe from the Transition menu.

3   Press the spacebar to play your slideshow, which now looks livelier with the new settings applied. But there is still room for improvements: For example, the image where two of the girls look away is not a good choice with which to start the slide show.

4   The second last picture looks like a better choice as first image of the show. Click its thumbnail, drag it to the left, and place it right in front of the first thumbnail. As a result, the first four images move back one position. To work with the thumbnail images in a larger panel, click the Quick Reorder button (⏏), located above the thumbnail images to the left. When done, click Back in the Quick Reorder panel.

Adding Extras

Now that you're happy with the picture order and transitions, let's increase the impact of the slide show by including some graphic elements. First, let's add a message with a speech bubble and text.

1   In the Slide Show Editor window, select the first thumbnail image in the row of thumbnail images near the bottom of the window.

2   Under Extras, select the graphics category, and then scroll down to Thought & Speech Bubbles. If necessary, click the triangle next to the name to show the available shapes. Click the first speech bubble icon and drag it near the first girl's head.

3   To change the size or shape of the bubble, position the pointer over one of the six handles located at the corners and sides of the bounding box, and when the pointer turns into a double arrow, drag to reduce the size or change the shape of the bubble. Try to size and shape the bubble as show in the illustration below. If necessary, click and drag the bubble to reposition it on the image.

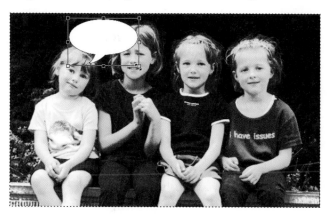

4   Under Extras, select the type category, and then locate the second T in the third row, a thin, black letter that represents the font Myriad Pro Condensed.

5   Drag the T onto the speech bubble in the Editor panel.

6   Click the Edit Text button in the Properties panel and type HELLO! in the Edit Text dialog box that appears. Then click OK.

7   Click and drag the text box to center the text in the speech bubble.

8   Now the first slide has a prominent message, but there is so much more you could do. Explore on your own! For example, add items to the last image from Costumes in the graphics category, to finish off your presentation with some fun touches.

9 When done, choose File > Save As, and type **4_Slideshow_work** as name in the Adobe Photoshop Elements dialog box. Then click Save.

Done! You've completed this lesson and have learned about some fun features. There are, as mentioned before, many more exciting templates to choose from and great projects ahead of you to be created.

Review

▶ **Review questions**

1　How do you create a photo project such as an online gallery, greeting card, or slide show?

2　How can you resize and reposition a photo when creating a greeting card?

3　What is an online gallery?

4　How can you change the order of your slides in a slide show?

▶ **Review answers**

1　To create a project in the Organizer, select an option in the Create panel of the Task pane, which then guides you through the creation process, offering several choices to personalize your project, such as specifying a template, layout, theme, and more.

2　Once you've selected a theme and a layout for the greeting card and clicked Done, an edit window opens with a bounding box around your photo. You can resize the photo by placing the pointer over a handle in the corners or the bounding box and dragging it to the desired position. When resizing a bounding box, the image is scaled proportionally by default. Click and drag the photo to reposition it.

3　An online gallery is a dynamic presentation of your images, which you can burn onto a CD, upload to Adobe Photoshop Services, or post to your Web site. You don't need to know anything about HTML programming to create a photo gallery—the Online Gallery wizard provides you with a wide variety of gallery styles from which you can select, and guides you through every step of the project.

4　One way to reorganize the order of slides is to click the thumbnail in your project bin, and then drag it to the right or left, until you've found the correct spot. You can also reorder your slides by clicking the Quick Reorder button, which is located above the thumbnail images to the left.

5 Printing, Sharing, and Exporting

In the previous lessons you've learned how to import and organize your photos and how to combine text and images to design stunning Creations. Naturally, you'd like to have printed copies of your favorite pictures and share your files with your friends and family.

In this lesson, you'll learn how to do the following:

- Print photos on your home printer.

- Order professionally printed photos online.

- Share photos in e-mail.

- Create a quick share flow.

- Use an online sharing service.

- Burn photos to CD or DVD.

- Export images for Web use.

Before you begin, make sure that you have correctly copied the Lessons folder from the CD in the back of this book onto your computer's hard disk. See "Copying the Classroom in a Book files" on page 3.

Getting started

For this lesson, you can use either a catalog you have created with your own pictures or the CIB Catalog you created at the start of the book. To use the CIB Catalog, follow these steps:

1   Start Photoshop Elements. In the Welcome Screen, click Organize in the row of shortcut buttons across the lower part of the Welcome Screen. If the CIB Catalog is open, skip to "About printing" on the next page. If the CIB Catalog is not open, complete the following steps.

2　Choose File > Catalog.

3　In the Catalog Manager dialog box, select the CIB Catalog under Catalogs, and then click Open.

If you do not see the CIB Catalog file, review the procedures found in "Getting Started." See "Copying the Lessons files from the CD" on page 3, and "Creating a catalog" on page 4.

About printing

Photoshop Elements provides several options for printing your photos. You can have photos professionally printed by online providers through Adobe Photoshop Services, or you can print your photos on your home printer. You can print individual photos, contact sheets (thumbnails of each selected photo), picture packages (a page of one or more photos printed at various sizes), or labels (arranging the photos on a grid for printing on commercially available label paper). Finally, you can print creations you've made in Photoshop Elements, such as photo albums, greeting cards, and calendars.

Printing individual photos

The Organizer helps you reduce waste of expensive photographic paper. You can print single or multiple images on the same page, arranging them on the paper in the sizes you want.

1　In the Organizer, select your favorite thumbnails. Click one thumbnail to select it, and then hold down Ctrl and click several others images you want to print.

2　Choose File > Print.

3　In the Print Photos dialog box, make the following adjustments:

- Under Select Printer, select an available printer.

- Under Select Type of Print, choose Individual Prints.

- Under Select Print Size and Options, select 3.5" x 5".

If a warning appears about print resolution, click OK to close it. Some of the sample files are provided at a low resolution, which is why you might get this warning.

- If selected, deselect the One Photo Per Page check box.

4   (Optional) Do any of the following:

• On the left side of the dialog box, select one of the thumbnails, and then click the Remove button (➖) at the bottom of the thumbnails column to remove that image from the set that will be printed.

• Click the Add button (➕) under the column of thumbnails. Select the Entire Catalog option, and then click the check box of any image that you want to add to the set to be printed. Click Done.

• If you have more pictures selected than fit on one page, click the arrows under the Print Preview in the middle of the dialog box, to see the other pages that will be printed.

Note: You can select only images that are part of the current catalog. If you want to add other pictures to the printing batch, you must first add them to the catalog, using one of the methods described earlier in this lesson.

5   Do one of the following:

• Click Cancel to close the dialog box without printing. This is recommended if you want to save your ink and paper for your own images.

• Click Print to actually print the pictures.

Printing a contact sheet

Contact sheets let you easily preview groups of images by displaying a series of thumbnail images on a single page.

1   In the Photo Browser, select one or more photos.

2   Choose File > Print.

Note: If you don't select specific photos before choosing Print, Photoshop Elements asks whether you want to print all photos in the Photo Browser.

3   In the Print Photos dialog box, choose a printer from the Select Printer menu.

4   Choose Contact Sheet from the Select Type of Print menu. The preview layout automatically uses all photos listed on the left side of the Print Photos dialog box. To remove a photo, select its thumbnail and click the Remove button.

5   For Columns, type **4** to specify the number of columns in the layout. You can specify between 1 and 9 columns.

The thumbnail size and number of rows are adjusted according to your choice. If the number of photos listed in the Print Photos dialog box exceeds the capacity of a single page, more pages are added to accommodate them.

6   To add text labels below each thumbnail, select any of the following:

• Date, to print the date embedded in the image.

• Caption, to print the caption text embedded in the file's metadata.

• Filename, to print the image file name.

• Page Numbers, to print page numbers at the bottom of each page (this option is only available if multiple contact sheets are printed).

Note: Words in the text label may be truncated, depending on the page setup and layout.

7   Click Print to print, or click Cancel.

Printing a Picture Package

Picture Package lets you place multiple copies of one or more photos on a single printed page. You can choose from a variety of size and placement options to customize your package layout.

1   Select one or more pictures from the browser, and then choose File > Print.

2   In the Print Photos dialog box, choose a printer from the Select Printer menu.

3   Choose Picture Package from the Select Type of Print menu. If a Printing Warning dialog box cautioning against enlarging pictures appears, click OK. You will print multiple smaller pictures.

4   Choose a layout from the Select a Layout menu, and select the Fill Page With First Photo check box.

Note: The options available under the Select a Layout menu depend on the paper size selected in the printer preferences. To change the printer preferences, click the button next to the Select Printer menu.

5   (Optional) Choose Icicles (or another border of your preference) from the Select a Frame menu. You can select only one border for the picture package.

💡 *To print the images listed in the dialog box on separate pages, click the Fill Page with First Photo option. You can use the Navigation buttons below the layout preview to view each layout.*

Note: *Depending on the layout you choose, the images are oriented to produce the optimum coverage of the printable area. This feature is automatic and cannot be overridden. You cannot rotate the images placed in the layout.*

6   To crop photos so they fit the layout size perfectly, click Crop to Fit.

Note: *If you want to add a photo to your picture package layout and it's not listed in the Print Photos dialog box, click the Add button and use the Add Photos dialog box to select the photos you want. Click Done to add the selected photos to the list in the Print Photos dialog box. To replace a photo in the layout, drag an image from the left side of the Print Photos dialog box over an image in the layout preview and release the mouse button.*

7   Click Print to print the package on your computer, or click Cancel.

Ordering professionally printed photos online

If you want highest quality prints of your photos—for your own enjoyment or to share with others—you can order professionally printed photos online. In this exercise you will learn how to order individual prints from the Organizer (a service available in the US, Canada, and Japan).

Note: *You must have an active Internet connection to order prints online.*

1   In the Organizer, select one or more pictures you would like to have professionally printed.

2   If the Quick Share palette is not already open in the Organize bin, choose Window > Quick Share to open it.

3   Drag the selected photos from the Browser view onto the words *Drag photos here to create an order* in the Quick Share palette.

The New Order Prints Recipient dialog box appears.

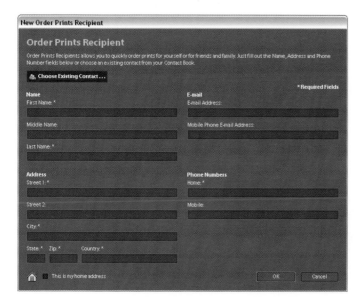

4　In the New Order Prints Recipient dialog box, enter all required information for the person to receive the printed photos. For this exercise, you can enter your own name, address, and home phone number (and select the This is my home address check box). Or, if you want to import contact information from an existing contact book entry, click the Choose Existing Contact button, select a contact from the list, and then click OK to close the Contact Book dialog box.

5　Click OK to close the New Order Prints Recipient dialog box.

A new target entry appears in the Quick Share palette. If you selected the This is my home address check box in the New Order Prints Recipient dialog box in step 4, you'll see a home icon next to the name of the target entry. The number in brackets next to the name indicates the number of selected photos for this print order.

6　In the Quick Share palette, double-click the name of the new target entry to open the Order Prints for *your name* dialog box. Do any of the following:

- Use the slider to increase or decrease the thumbnail image size.

- Select one or more photos and click Remove Selected Photo(s).

- Click Remove All to remove all photos from the current order.

7 When done, click Close to close the dialog box without confirming the order yet.

8 (Optional) Drag additional photos from the Browser view onto the same target entry in the Quick Share palette:

9 In the Quick Share palette, click the Order button on the right side of the target entry.

10 In the Welcome to Adobe Photoshop Services dialog box, do one of the following:

• If you are already an Ofoto or EasyShare Gallery member, click Sign in, and then use the e-mail address and password associated with your existing online account to sign in.

• Create a new account by entering your first name, e-mail address, and a password of at least six characters. If you agree with the Terms of Service select the respective check box under Create Account, and then click Next.

11 In the Review Order dialog box, do any of the following:

• Click Change quantities or sizes to change the quantity or size of each photo in your order.

• Click Remove under a thumbnail image in the list on the left side of the dialog box to remove a print from your order.

• Review the information under Order Summary and Delivery Information.

12 When done reviewing your order, click Checkout:

13 If you wanted to proceed with an order, you would now provide your credit card details in the Billing Information dialog box and review the information under Billing Address and Order Summary. Then, starting the processing of your order—including charging your credit card!—would only be one Place Order click away. But for this exercise, click Cancel if you don't want to order any prints. In the dialog box that appears, click OK to confirm that you want to stop using this service. Right-click on the target name in the Order Prints palette, and then choose Cancel Order from the context menu. Click Yes to confirm canceling the order in the alert dialog box.

About sharing

In Lesson 1 you have learned how to use the Organizer's e-mail function, to create versions of your photos that are optimized to be sent as e-mail attachments. See "Sharing photos in e-mail" on page 26. Instead of sending photos as simple e-mail attachments, you can use the Photo Mail option to embed your photos in the body of an e-mail, using colorful custom layouts. To share items other than photos—like slide shows, photo galleries, or flipbooks—you generally have a choice of output options during the creation process.

Using Photo Mail

1   In the Organizer, select one or more photos that you would like to share via e-mail with your friends or family.

2   In the Share panel of the Task pane, click the Photo Mail button.

3   Next to Items, select the Include captions check box, and then click Next.

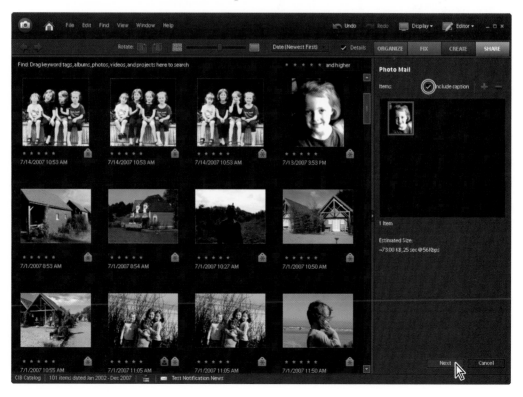

4 Under Message, select and delete the "Here are the photos...." text and type a message of your own.

5 Select a recipient from the list under Select Recipients. (If you didn't work through Lesson 1 and your recipient list is still empty, click the Edit Contact Book button (⊕), and then create a new entry using the Contact Book dialog box).

6 Click Next.

7 In the Stationery & Layouts Wizard dialog box, select a stationery format appropriate for the selected photos: Click on a category name to show the available design choices, and then select a stationery type from the submenu. A preview of your e-mail body will appear on the right side of the dialog box.

8 Click Next Step. Customize the layout by selecting an option under Photo Size and under Layout. Click the message text to edit it. Click next to the photo (either left or right or under the photo, depending on your layout selected in step 7) to edit the caption text.

9   Click Next.

Photoshop Elements opens your default e-mail application and creates an e-mail message with your design in the body of the message. You can send Photo Mail through Outlook Express, Outlook, or Adobe E-mail Service.

10   Switch back to Photoshop Elements (Organizer).

Creating a quick share flow

If you find yourself sending the same kind of documents to the same group of people on a regular basis, then setting up a quick share target can help you automate your work considerably. For example, if you frequently (or even only occasionally) send your family an e-mail message with selected photos from each vacation, only once do you need to set up the quick share target (including information such as the mailing list and the desired image size for the photos), and then reuse these settings again and again by simply dropping photos on the quick share target.

While you can create a new order prints target by clicking the New button in the Quick Share palette, you can create a quick share target only from within the respective workflow. In the following steps you will set up a quick share target to send photos to a group of people as an e-mail attachment.

1   In the Photo Browser of the Organizer, select several photos of your choice.

2   In the Share panel of the Task pane, click the E-mail Attachments button.

3   Select Very Small (320 x 240 px) from the Maximum Photo Size menu (a good choice to keep the overall file size small if you want to send multiple images via e-mail) and adjust the image quality using the Quality slider (the higher the quality the longer the download time). The resulting file size and download time for a typical 56 Kbps dial-up modem are estimated and displayed for your reference. When done, click Next.

4   Under Message, select and delete the "Here are the photos...." text and type a message of your own.

5   Under Select Recipients, click to select the check boxes next to the recipients you want to include in this quick share target.

6   Under Save as Quick Share Flow?, select Yes, and then enter a descriptive name for this quick share target.

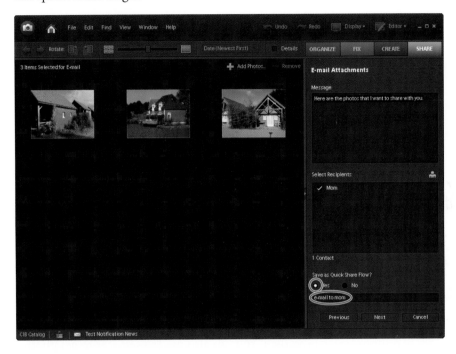

7   Click Next.

Your default e-mail application opens and creates an e-mail message with the selected photos attached in the selected image quality and size. You can further edit the message and Subject line if you want. When you are finished and ready to send the e-mail, make sure that you are connected to the Internet, either click Send if you want to send an actual e-mail, or close the message without saving or sending it.

8   Switch back to Photoshop Elements (Organizer). In the Quick Share palette, notice the new e-mail attachments quick share target. Select one or more photos in the Photo Browser and drop the selection onto this quick share target.

9   (Optional). Drop additional photos onto this quick share target. The number in brackets next to the name indicates the number of selected photos for this quick share target.

10   When done, click the E-mail button in the quick share target.

With just one click your default e-mail application opens and creates an e-mail message with the selected photos attached in the chosen image quality and size, ready to be send out.

11   Close your e-mail application, and then switch back to Photoshop Elements (Organizer).

Using an online sharing service

You can use Adobe Photoshop Services in Photoshop Elements to send images and creations to online service providers. You can also use the services to get photos.

1   In the Photo Browser of the Organizer, select the photos you wish to share.

2   In the Share panel of the Task pane, click the More Options button, and then choose Share with Kodak Easyshare Gallery from the menu to access the Kodak® EasyShare Gallery.

3   If the Welcome to Adobe Photoshop Services dialog box appears, do one of the following:

- If you are already an Ofoto or EasyShare Gallery member, click Sign in, and then use the e-mail address and password associated with your existing online account to sign in.

- Create a new account by entering your first name, e-mail address, and a password of at least six characters. If you agree with the Terms of Service, select the respective check box under Create Account, and then click Next.

Note: If you are still signed in to the Adobe Photoshop Services from the previous exercise, you don't need to sign in again. Just click Next to continue.

4   In the Share Online dialog box, click to select the Add New Address option.

5   In the Add Address dialog box, complete the address information for the person with whom you will share the photos, and then click Next.

6   In the Share Online dialog box, select the newly added address book check box. Under Message, type **Photos** in the subject field and type **Enjoy!** in the message field. Then, click Next.

Your photos are being uploaded.

7   In the Share Online Confirmation dialog box, click Done. Or, click Order Prints if you want to purchase prints of your photos, and then follow the on-screen directions.

An e-mail will be sent to the recipient you've specified in step 6, containing a Web link where the photos can be viewed online in a slide show.

About exporting

Even though there are a variety of ways to share your photos and creations using commands in Photoshop Elements, there may be situations where you want to export a copy of your files to use in another program. In the Organizer, you can move or copy your files to a CD or DVD. In the Editor, you can export you photos optimized for use in a Web design application.

Burning photos to CD or DVD

Use the Make a CD/DVD command in the Organizer to copy a set of photos to a CD or DVD. For instance, you might want to give your photos to a friend, or backup only selected images. Or, use the Copy/Move to Removable Disk to copy or move photos to any storage device—including hard disk, USB stick, network drive, or CD/DVD writer—attached to your computer.

Note: To make a full or incremental backup of your entire catalog, use the Backup Catalog to CD, DVD or Hard Drive command.

1   Make sure you have a CD or DVD drive with writable media connected to your computer.

2   In the Photo Browser, select the items you want to burn to a CD or DVD.

3   Choose File > Make a CD/DVD.

If you haven't selected any files, you'll see a dialog box giving you the option of selecting all files in the Photo Browser.

4   In the Make a CD/DVD dialog box, select a destination drive, and then click OK to actually copy your files to a writable CD or DVD. Or, click Cancel to exit the Make a CD/DVD dialog box without copying any files.

5   In the Photo Browser, select the items you want to copy or move.

6   Choose File > Copy/Move to Removable Disk.

The Copy/Move to Removable Disk wizard appears.

7   If selected, deselect the Move Files check box under Offline Media.

Note: Choosing the Move Files option deletes the original files from your hard disk after they are copied to the new location, keeping only a smaller low-resolution proxy file in the catalog. This is useful if you want to save hard disk space on your computer and only need to access the original files occasionally.

8   Under Stacks and Version Sets, you have the choice to copy/move only the first file or all files in a stack or version set. These options are dimmed, if you don't have any stacks or version sets in your selection of photos.

9   Click Next.

10   Select a destination drive in the Destination Settings dialog box. If you want to specify a subfolder on the destination drive as target location, click Browse, and then select the folder in the Browse For Folder dialog box.

11   Click Done to actually copy your files to the target location. Or, click Cancel to exit the Copy/Move to Removable Disk wizard without copying or moving any files.

> *Using the File > Export > As New File(s) command enables you to export photos not only in the original file format, but also in JPEG, PNG, TIFF, or PSD file format, along with options for images size, location, and custom file name.*

Saving copies of the images for Web use

Your final task in this lesson is to convert a file to JPEG format so it can be shared on a Web page. The JPEG file format reduces the file size and can be displayed by Web browsers such as Internet Explorer, which makes it an efficient file format for Web use. If your file contains multiple layers, the conversion to the JPEG file format will flatten them into one inseparable layer.

Here, you'll use the Save for Web feature, which enables you to tweak the export settings while comparing the original image file with the proposed Web version of the image.

1   In the Photo Browser, select a photo you want to save for Web use.

2   Click the Editor button (📝) located near the top right corner of the Organizer window, and then choose Quick Fix, Full Edit, or Guided Edit from the menu. Or, click the Quick Fix, Full Edit, or Guided Edit button in the Fix panel of the Task pane.

3   Wait until the Editor workspace has loaded, and then choose File > Save for Web.

4   In the Save For Web dialog box, choose Fit on Screen from the Zoom menu in the lower left corner of the dialog box.

Note: When previewing images using Save for Web, you can use the Zoom tool (🔍) in the upper left corner of the dialog box to zoom in, or zoom out by holding down Alt key when

clicking. When zoomed in, use the Hand tool (🖐) to drag both images at once, so that you see the same details in both views.

5   Under the two views of the image, notice the file-size information. The image on the left displays the file size of the original document.

6   On the right side of the dialog box, select JPEG Medium in the Preset menu. Notice the change in file size for the JPEG image on the right side of the dialog box.

7   Under New Size, select Constrain Proportions and type **300** in the Width field. Because you selected Constrain Proportions, the Height automatically changes to keep the image proportional.

8   In the New Size section of the Save for Web dialog box, click the Apply button. Again notice the change in the file size displayed beneath the JPEG view of the image. If necessary, choose Fit on Screen from the Zoom menu.

Note: If you need to reduce the file size even more, you can select JPEG Low, which reduces the file size by discarding more image data and further compressing the image. You can select intermediate levels between these options by changing the Quality value, either by typing a different number or by clicking the arrow and dragging the slider.

9   Click OK and in the Save Optimized As dialog box, navigate to the My CIB Work folder and add **_Work** to the end of the file name. Click Save.

Converting the files to the JPEG format reduces the file size by using JPEG compression and discarding some of the data, based upon the setting you select.

10   Back in the Editor, choose File > Close without saving any changes.

Congratulations! You've completed this lesson and should now have a good understanding of the basics of printing, sharing, and exporting.

In this lesson, you have seen how to set up single or multiple images for printing on your home printer and how to order professionally printed photos online. You've learned how to share photos using Photo Mail or an online sharing service and you've seen how a quick share flow can automate tasks you perform frequently. Finally, you've exported photos for backup purpose and for Web use.

Review

> ## Review questions

1 How do you print multiple images on a single sheet of paper?

2 What is Photo Mail?

3 What is a quick share flow?

4 What command can you use to backup all photos in your catalog to a CD or DVD?

5 Is the Save for Web command also available in Quick Fix mode?

> ## Review answers

1 All multi-photo printing with Photoshop Elements is done in the Organizer, although you can also start the process in the Editor. You start by selecting the photo or photos you want to print and choosing File > Print. Then, deselect the One Photo Per Page check box.

2 Instead of sending photos as simple e-mail attachments, you can use the Photo Mail option to embed your photos in the body of an e-mail, using colorful custom layouts. You can send Photo Mail through Outlook Express, Outlook, or Adobe E-mail Service.

3 A quick share flow can help you automate tasks you perform frequently. Save your settings as a quick share target from within the respective workflow—for example, when sending photos to a group of people as an e-mail attachment—and then perform the same task again by dropping photos onto the quick share target in the Quick Share palette.

4 In the Organizer, choose File > Backup Catalog. After the first full backup, you can choose to perform only an incremental backup. To copy or move only selected files in your catalog, use the File > Copy/Move Offline command.

5 Yes, the Save for Web command is available in all three modes of the Editor, Quick Fix, Full Edit, and Guided Edit.

6 Adjusting Color in Images

Color casts, or unwanted imbalances in the color of an image, can be caused by the light source, incorrect camera exposure settings, or other issues relating to the input device. Photoshop Elements provides several tools for fixing color problems in your photos. You can also use these tools creatively to vary the color of an object in a picture.

In this lesson, you will learn how to do the following:

- Correct color problems in Guided Edit mode.
- Auto-correct images in either Quick Fix or Full Edit mode.
- Use individual automatic options to improve images.
- Adjust skin tones.
- Correct an image using Smart Fix.
- Apply the Color Variations feature to shift color balance.
- Removing red eyes in the Editor.
- Make and save selection areas for future use.
- Apply color adjustments to a selected image area.
- Troubleshoot common problems when printing color pictures.
- Work with color management.

This lesson shows you many different ways to change the color balance in your pictures, beginning with the one-step correction features. From there, you'll discover advanced features and adjustment techniques that can be mastered easily.

Most people need at least an hour and a half to complete the work in this lesson. Several different projects are involved and you can do them all in one session or in several sessions.

In this lesson, you will use the CIB Catalog you created earlier in the "Getting Started" section at the beginning of this book. If the CIB Catalog is not currently open in the Organizer, choose File > Catalog, and then select and open the CIB Catalog.

This lesson focuses primarily on the Editor and also builds on the skills and concepts covered in earlier lessons.

Before you begin, make sure that you have correctly copied the Lessons folder from the CD in the back of this book onto your computer's hard disk. See "Copying the Classroom in a Book files" on page 3.

Note: As you gain advanced skills in Photoshop Elements 6.0, you may require additional information about issues and problems. For help with common problems you might have when completing lessons in this book, see "Why won't Photoshop Elements do what I tell it to do?" later in this lesson.

Getting started

Before you start working, take a few moments to make sure that your work area and palettes are set up to match the illustrations in this section.

1   Start Photoshop Elements in Full Edit mode by selecting Edit in the Photoshop Elements Welcome Screen. If the Organizer is already open, click the Editor button (🖅) located near the top right corner of the Organizer window, and then choose Full Edit from the menu.

2   In Full Edit, use the Window menu to make the Tools palette, Palette Bin, and Project Bin visible. In both Full Edit and Quick Fix modes, you can expand collapsed palettes in the Palette Bin by clicking the arrow beside the palette name on the palette title bar.

Note: For instructions on how to add or remove palettes from the Full Edit Palette Bin, see "Using the Palette Bin" in Lesson 1, "A Quick Tour of Photoshop Elements." You cannot add or remove palettes in Quick Fix mode.

In this lesson, you will be using the Editor in Full Edit mode, Quick Fix mode, and Guided Edit mode.

Editor workspace in Full Edit mode.

Editor workspace in Quick Fix mode.

Editor workspace in Guided Edit mode.

Fixing photographs automatically

You may have noticed that not all the photographs used for the lessons in this book are of professional quality. Many of the pictures were selected to illustrate typical challenges that people might face when attempting to make the most of their photographs.

Batch-processing multiple files

Photoshop Elements can fix multiple photographs in batch mode. In this section, you'll apply automatic fixes to all the image files used in this lesson. You'll save those fixed files as copies of the originals so that you can compare the results at the end of each project.

1   In the Editor, choose File > Process Multiple Files. The Process Multiple Files dialog box opens.

2   In the Process Multiple Files dialog box, set the source and destination folders as follows:

•   Choose Folder from the Process Files From menu.

- Under Source, click the Browse button. Find and select the Lesson06 folder in the Lessons folder. Click OK to close the Browse for Folder dialog box.

- Under Destination, click Browse. Then, find and select the My CIB Work folder that you created at the start of the book. Click OK to close the Browse for Folder dialog box.

3   Under File Naming, select Rename Files. Select Document Name in the first field, and type **_Autofix** in the second field. This adds the appendix "_Autofix" to the existing document name as the files are saved in the My CIB Work folder.

4   Under Quick Fix on the right side of the dialog box, select all four options: Auto Levels, Auto Contrast, Auto Color, and Sharpen.

5   Review all selections in the dialog box, comparing them to the following illustration. Make sure that the Resize Images and the Convert Files to options are not selected.

Note: While performing the next step, if an error message appears saying that some files couldn't be processed, ignore it. This might be caused by a hidden file that is not an image, so it has no effect on the success of your project. If an error message appears saying that files are missing, that means that the Lessons folder has been moved or was not expanded

correctly. See "Copying the Classroom in a Book files" on page 3 and redo that procedure, following the instructions exactly.

6 When you are sure that all selections are correct, click OK.

Photoshop Elements goes to work, automatically opening and closing image windows. All you need to do is sit back and wait for the process to finish.

Note: You can use Windows Explorer to see the images fixed by Quick Fix or, after adding them to your catalog as explained in the next section, in the Photo Browser of Photoshop Elements. For more information on the Photo Browser, see Photoshop Elements Help.

Adding the corrected files to the Organizer

The Save, Save As, and Save Optimized As dialog boxes all have an Include in Organizer option that is selected by default. When you use the Process Multiple Files feature, this option isn't part of the process, so you must add the files to the Organizer manually.

1 In the Editor, click the Organizer button (⊞) to open the Organizer workspace.

2 In the Organizer, choose File > Get Photos and Videos > From Files and Folders.

3 In the dialog box that appears, locate and open the My CIB Work folder.

4 Ctrl-click or drag-select all five _Autofix files.

5 Select Automatically Fix Red Eyes, deselect Automatically Suggest Photo Stacks, and then click Get Photos.

6   The Import Attached Keyword Tags dialog box opens. Click OK without selecting any keyword tags, as you'll be adding keyword tags manually in the next few steps.

7   If the Auto Red Eye Fix Complete dialog box appears, click OK.

8   If a message appears reminding you that only the new photos will appear, click OK. The Organizer displays the newly added image thumbnails.

9   Choose Edit > Select All, or press Ctrl+A.

10   If necessary, click the triangle next to Imported Keyword Tags in the Keyword Tags palette to show the imported keyword tags. Scroll down to find the Lesson 6 keyword tag. Then, drag the Lesson 6 keyword tag to any of the selected image thumbnails to apply it to all selected images.

11   Click the Show All button above the Photo Browser.

Now you are ready to discover other methods for correcting color.

Using Guided Edit for editing

If you are new to digital photography, Guided Edit is the place to start for fixing common image problems. But by using the Guided Edit mode, even more experienced users can pick up some tricks, or just enjoy the simplicity of working in that mode.

Removing a color cast using Guided Edit

One of the images in the Lesson 6 folder, the picture of three vases, has a very obvious color cast. The picture was taken indoors with inadequate lighting. You will remove that color cast using the Guided Edit mode of the Editor.

1   If the Organizer is not currently active, switch to it now.

2   In the Keyword Tags palette, click the Find box next to the Lesson 6 keyword tag.

3   Select the original picture of the three vases, 06_01.jpg, to make it active. Pay attention not to confuse the original file with the file 06_01_Autofix.jpg, where color correction—among other things—has already been applied.

Note: To show the file names in the Photo Browser, choose View > Show File Names.

4   Click the Editor button (📝) located near the top right corner of the Organizer window, and then choose Guided Edit from the menu.

5   Wait until the Editor workspace has loaded with the image of the three vases open in Guided Edit mode.

6   If necessary, click the triangle next to Color Correction under What would you like to do. Then, click to select Remove a Color Cast in the group of Color Correction tasks.

7 Click the button near the bottom of the Guided Edit panel to select Before & After - Horizontal as display mode.

8 Read the instructions under Correct Color Cast. Then, using the Color Cast Eyedropper tool, click near the top left corner of the Before image to remove the color cast. Notice the change in the After image.

9 (Optional) If you are not satisfied with the result, click the Undo button (↰) next to the menu bar of the organizer window, and then click a different area in the Before image. Or, to clear the Undo/Redo history and start all over with the original version of the image, click the Reset button in the Guided Edit panel.

10 When you are satisfied with the result of the color correction in the After image, click Done near the bottom of the Guided Edit panel of the Tasks panel.

Adjusting lighting using Guided Edit

As with many images, this image has more than just one imperfection. After the color cast has been removed, the image looks as if it could benefit from some lighting adjustment.

1 If necessary, click the triangle next to Lighting and Exposure under What would you like to do. Then, click to select Lighten or Darken in the group of Lighting and Exposure tasks.

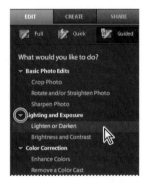

2 In the panel that appears, click the Auto button under Lighten or Darken a Photo. Notice the immediate big improvement to the image quality.

3 Use the sliders for Lighten Shadows, Darken Highlights, and Midtone Contrast to further adjust the lighting of the image. We used a value of 30 for Lighten Shadows, left the value for Darken Highlights at 0, and used a value of 32 for Midtone Contrast. Your choices may vary, based on your results from the color correction as well as your preferences for the appearance of the final image.

4 When you are satisfied with the result of the lighting adjustment in the After image, click Done near the bottom of the Guided Edit panel of the Tasks panel.

5 (Optional) Select Sharpen Photo in the group of Basic Photo Edits under What would you like to do. Click the Auto button under Sharpen Photo. Use the slider to manually adjust sharpening to your liking, and then click Done.

6 Choose File > Save As. In the Save As dialog box, navigate to and open the My CIB Work folder, leave the JPEG file format selected, name the file **06_01_Guided**, select Include in the Organizer, deselect Save in Version Set with Original, and then click Save.

7 Click OK in the JPEG Options dialog box without making any changes.

8 In the Editor, choose File > Close, and then switch back to the Organizer.

9 In the Organizer, click the Show All button above the Photo Browser, and then scroll down to find the newly added file 06_01_Guided.jpg and apply to it the Lesson 6 keyword tag.

With just a few clicks you have dramatically improved the quality of the image. To get good results using Guided Edit you don't have to have prior experience in using an image editor. Guided Edit even offers two Guided Activities—called "Touch Up Scratches, Blemishes or Tear Marks" and "Guide for Editing a Photo"—taking you step-by-step in the recommended order through several image editing tasks to get professional results. When you are ready to move on to the next level of photo editing there is Quick Fix, which you will use in the next exercise.

Using Quick Fix for editing

Quick Fix conveniently assembles many of the basic photo fixing tools in Photoshop Elements. If one control doesn't work for your image, click the Reset button and try another one. You can also adjust your image using the slider controls, whether you've used the Quick Fix feature or not.

Applying individual automatic adjustments

When you apply automatic fixes to images using the Process Multiple Files dialog box, you only briefly see the before, during, and after versions of the file. In this project, you'll apply individual aspects of automatic fixing, one at a time. This is useful because it enables you to see how the different phases affect the image, and also enables you to make individual adjustments to the correction process.

Opening image files for Quick Fix editing

You'll use the same technique you learned in Lesson 2 for using the Organizer to find and open files for editing in Quick Fix mode.

1   If the Organizer is not currently active, switch to it now.

2   In the Keyword Tags palette, click the Find box next to the Lesson 6 keyword tag.

3   Select the original version of the image with three vases, 06_01.jpg.

Note: To show the file names in the Photo Browser, choose View > Show File Names.

4   Click the Editor button (☑) located near the top right corner of the Organizer window, and then choose Quick Fix from the menu.

5   From the View menu in the lower left corner of the image window, choose Before & After - Horizontal.

Note: You can change from Before & After - Horizontal to Before & After - Vertical, if you prefer that arrangement. The horizontal view shows the before and after versions of the image side by side. The vertical view shows them one above the other.

Using Smart Fix

With Photoshop Elements in Quick Fix mode, you see four palettes in the Palette Bin on the right—General Fixes, Lighting, Color, and Sharpen. In the General Fixes palette, the first option available is called Smart Fix.

Smart Fix corrects overall color balance and improves shadow and highlight detail in your image. As with other automatic fixes in Quick Fix mode, you can click the Auto button to apply these corrections automatically. You can also move the Amount slider to vary the degree of the adjustment. Or, as in the following steps, you can use a combination of both adjustments.

1   In the Palette Bin, under General Fixes, click the Auto button for Smart Fix. Notice the immediate effect on the image.

2   Now, move the Amount slider to change the adjustments of the color balance and detail in your image. You can determine which adjustment works best for you. In our example the slider is in the middle.

3   Click the Commit button (✔) in the General Fixes palette title bar to commit the changes.

Applying other automatic fixes

Additional automatic fixes are available in the Palette Bin under Lighting, Color, and Sharpen.

1 In the Palette Bin, under Lighting, click the Auto button for Levels. You may need to open a palette to see the Auto button. Depending upon the adjustment you made in Smart Fix, you may or may not see a big shift in the lighting of this image.

2 One at a time, click the Auto buttons for Contrast, Color, and Sharpen, noticing the difference in the image with each adjustment.

3 (Optional) Experiment with the adjustment sliders in each section. Click the Commit button (✔) in the respective title bar to commit the changes. Click the Reset button above the After image if you want to undo your modifications and start over again using the original version of the image.

4 When you have obtained your preferred result, choose File > Save As. In the Save As dialog box, navigate to and open the My CIB Work folder, rename the file **06_01_ Quick** and select the JPEG format. Select Include in the Organizer. If Save in Version Set with Original is selected, deselect it. Click Save.

5 When the JPEG Options dialog box appears, select High from the Quality menu, and then click OK.

6 In the Editor, choose File > Close, and then switch back to the Organizer.

7 In the Organizer, find the newly added file 06_01_Quick.jpg and apply the Lesson 6 keyword tag to it.

Comparing methods of fixing color

The automatic correction features in Photoshop Elements do an excellent job of bringing out the best in most photographs. But each photograph is unique, and so are the potential problems. Some photographs don't respond well to automatic fixes and require a more hands-on approach to color correction.

Photoshop Elements offers many ways to deal with color correction. The more procedures you master, the more likely you'll be able meet the challenge of fixing a difficult photograph. In this section, you'll study three different methods for correcting a color problem, and compare the results.

Creating extra working copies of an image

You're going to compare three approaches to color correction, so you'll need three copies of the same photograph.

Note: By now, you should have mastered the procedure for using keyword tags to locate the files you need in the Organizer. From now on, the instructions for opening files will be summarized rather than explained in detail.

1   In the Organizer, use the Lesson 6 keyword tag to find the file 06_02.jpg. Pay attention not to confuse the original file with the file 06_02_Autofix.jpg.

2   Select the file 06_02.jpg in the Photo Browser, and then click the Editor button ( ) located near the top right corner of the Organizer window and choose Quick Fix from the menu.

3   In Quick Fix mode of the Editor, choose File > Duplicate. In the Duplicate Image dialog box, click OK to accept the default name, 06_02 copy.jpg.

4   Repeat Step 3 to create another duplicate, 06_02 copy 2.jpg.

Leave all three copies of the image file open for the next procedures. You can tell that the files are open because the thumbnails appear in the Project Bin at the bottom of your screen.

Automatically fixing color

At the beginning of this lesson, you applied all four Quick Fix options to each of the images used in this lesson and saved the results in a separate location. In this procedure, you'll apply just one type of Quick Fix.

1   In the Project Bin, double-click the 06_02.jpg thumbnail to make it the active file. To see the file name, hover with the pointer over the thumbnail in the Project Bin.

2   In the Color palette, click Auto to fix only the color.
Compare the Before and After views of the file.

3   Choose File > Save, saving the file in the My CIB Work folder and in JPEG format, changing the name to **06_02_Work**. Make sure Save in Version Set with Original is deselected. Click Save, leaving all other options in the Save and JPEG Options dialog box unchanged.

Adjusting the results of an automatic fix

In this procedure, you'll experiment with one of the sliders in the Quick Fix palettes.

1   In the Photo Bin, double-click the 06_02 copy thumbnail to make it the active file.

2 Click the Auto button for Color. The results are the same as you had in the previous procedure.

3 Drag the Temperature slider a small amount to the right.

This makes the image look warmer, reducing the blue and green tones while enhancing yellows, reds, and oranges.

4 Examine the results, paying particular attention to the skin tones.

5 Readjust the Temperature slider until you are satisfied with the realistic balance, achieving warm skin tones without the rest of the image getting too red. Then, click the Commit button (✔) at the top of the Color palette. In the sample shown, we moved the Temperature slider only slightly to the right.

Note: If you aren't happy with the results and want to start over, click Cancel (⊘) on the Color palette tab. If you decide to undo the color fix after you click the Commit button, click the Reset button above the image. This restores the image to its original condition.

6   Choose File > Save, saving the file in the My CIB Work folder and in JPEG format, changing the name to **06_02 copy_Work**. Notice that the Save in Version Set with Original option is not available, since the 06_02 copy.jpg file has not been added to the catalog. Click Save, leaving all other options in the Save and JPEG Options dialog boxes unchanged.

About viewing modes and image window arrangements

When you work in Quick Fix mode, only one image file appears in the work area, regardless of how many files are open. The inactive, open files appear as thumbnails in the Photo Bin but not in the work area.

When you work in Full Edit mode, other arrangements are possible. You can usually adjust the size and placement of image windows in the work area. If you can't arrange individual windows freely, your view is probably set to Maximize Mode. If opening or closing some files causes unexpected rearrangements of image windows, your view is probably set to Tile.

Maximize Mode fills the work area with the active image window, so it's the only image you can see.

Tile resizes and arranges all open images so that the image windows cover the work area. If Tile mode is active when you close an image file or open a new one, Photoshop Elements will rearrange the image windows in tile formation.

Cascade enables you to resize, arrange, or minimize files.

There are two ways to switch from one mode to another.

• Use the Window > Images menu and choose the arrangement you want: Maximize Mode, Tile, or Cascade. Or, if there is a check mark on the Maximize Mode command, choosing Maximize Mode again deactivates it and switches to the mode you were using previously.

• Select an icon on the far right end of the window title bar.

The available icons vary, depending on which viewing mode is active, and on the size of the work area on your monitor. If the work area is reduced, these icons may not appear.

A   B

A. Switch to Maximize Mode. **B.** *Switch to previous mode.*

For more information, see "Working in the Editor: Viewing images in the Editor" in Adobe Photoshop Elements Help.

Tweaking results from automatic fix

The top six commands in the Enhance menu apply the same changes as the Auto buttons in the Quick Fix palettes. These commands are available in both Quick Fix and Full Edit, but not in Guided Edit.

Both Quick Fix and Full Edit offer other methods of enhancing color in images. These are found in the lower half of the Enhance menu. In this procedure, you use a manual option to tweak the results produced by an automatic fix button.

1 In the Photo Bin, double-click the 06_02 copy 2 thumbnail to make it the active file.

2 In the Color palette, click Auto to apply the automatic color correction.

3 Choose Enhance > Adjust Color > Color Variations.

4 In the lower left area of the Color Variations dialog box, make sure that Midtones is selected, and that the Amount slider is approximately centered. Click the Decrease Blue thumbnail once, and then Click OK:

This reduces the amount of blue in the images, probably even too much. To try again, using a smaller value or a different combination of adjustments, you can undo the changes and start again. (Choose Edit > Undo Color Variations, and then try again, starting with Step 3.)

5   Choose File > Save As, and navigate to the My CIB Work folder. Rename the file **06_02 copy 2_Work**, and select the JPEG format. Click Save, leaving all other options in the Save and JPEG Options dialog boxes unchanged.

Comparing results

As you can tell by viewing the Photo Bin, all three copies of the image are open. Now you'll compare them to the autofix file you processed at the beginning of this lesson.

1   Choose File > Open. Locate and open the My CIB Work folder. Select the file 06_02_Autofix, and then click Open.

2   In the Edit panel of the Tasks pane, select the Full tab (📝) to switch to the Full Edit mode.

3   Choose Window > Images > Tile, if it's not already selected.

4   Use the Zoom tool and the Hand tool to select an area of interest in one of the images, and then choose Window > Images > Match Zoom and Windows > Images > Match Location.

5   In the toolbox, select the Zoom tool (🔍).

6   In the tool options bar, select Zoom Out.

7   Do one of the following:

•   Click in the active image window until you can see the entire photo. Then, choose Window > Images > Match Zoom.

•   In the tool options bar, select Zoom In. If it's not already selected, select Zoom All Windows in the tool options bar, and then click in the active image window until you can see the entire photo.

Note: At any given time there is only one active window. Look at the text in the title bars of the open image windows; the text is dimmed on all inactive image windows.

8   In the toolbox, select the Hand tool (✋).

9   In the tool options bar, select Scroll All Windows.

10   Click and drag within the active window to examine different areas of the image. Compare the four images and decide which looks best. Then, drag any corner edge of the image window to resize it so it fills the space and turn off Tile mode.

11   Choose View > Fit on Screen to enlarge the image so it fits in the window.

💡 *Press Ctrl-Tab or Ctrl-Shift-Tab to cycle through all open windows.*

Adjusting skin tones

Sometimes the combination of ambient light and surrounding color can cause skin tones in your image to be tinted with unwanted color. Photoshop Elements offers a unique solution, in both the Full Edit and Quick Fix modes (but not in Guided Edit).

To adjust color for skin tones do the following:

1   Choose Enhance > Adjust Color > Adjust Color for Skin Tone.

2   Make sure the Preview option is selected in the Adjust Color for Skin Tone dialog box. Then, with the eyedropper cursor (✐) that appears when you hover over the image in the Editor window, click an area of the kid's skin, for example on the face.

Photoshop Elements automatically adjusts the entire photo using the color of the child's skin as reference.

3   If you're unsatisfied with the correction, click on a different point in the image or move the Tan, Blush, and Temperature sliders to achieve the desired result.

> 💡 *While the Adjust Color for Skin Tone dialog box is open, you can switch to the Zoom tool or Hand tool in the Editor window to focus on a different area of the image. Switch back to the Eyedropper tool when you want to click another skin area in the image.*

4   When you're satisfied with the skin tone, click OK to close the Adjust Color for Skin Tone dialog box, and then choose File > Close All. When asked, do not save the changes.

Working with red eye

Red eye occurs when a camera flash is reflected off the retina so that the dark center of the eye looks bright red. Photoshop Elements can automatically fix red eye when you bring photos into the Organizer. Just select Automatically Fix Red Eyes in the Get Photos dialog box when you import your photos (see the *Automatically Fixing Red Eyes* sidebar in Lesson 2). Or, you can apply the red eye fix command to images already in your catalog. In Lesson 8 you will learn how red eyes can be fixed directly in the Organizer, but here we will use the tools available in the Editor.

Using automatic Red Eye Fix in the Editor

Just as you automatically corrected color balance earlier in this lesson with Smart Fix, you can also apply an automatic red eye correction in Quick Fix mode. This method might not successfully remove red eye from all images, but Photoshop Elements provides other options.

In this procedure, you will be fixing red eyes in the Quick Fix mode of the Editor. But first, you'll use the Organizer to find the image to be fixed in your catalog.

1   In the Editor, click the Organizer button to load the Organizer workspace. If necessary, click the Show All button above the Photo Browser.

2   In the Keywords Tags palette, click the Find box next to the Lesson 6 keyword tag. For this exercise, you will be working on the uncorrected picture of the child with the red eyes, 06_03.jpg. Do not confuse this file with the version that has the autofix or auto red eye fix applied. If necessary, choose View > Show File Names.

3   In the Photo Browser, click the 06_03.jpg image to select it. Then, click the Editor button located near the top right corner of the Organizer window and choose Quick Fix from the menu that appears. Wait until the Editor has finished opening the file.

4   Select Before & After - Vertical from the View menu below the preview pane. Use the Zoom and Hand tools to focus on the eye area in the image.

5   In the Palette Bin, under General Fixes, click the Auto button next to Red Eye Fix. There is no slider available for this correction. As you can see, the Auto correction does a reasonably good job, but in this admittedly difficult case it also affects the color of the iris.

6   Click the Reset button above the edited image to revert the photo to its state before the Auto Red Eye Fix was applied.

The Auto Red Eye Fix feature works well for most images, but if you want more control in some cases, then the Red Eye Removal tool is just what you need.

Note: The Auto Red Eye Fix correction is also available as a command under the Enhance menu, along with other automatic correction controls like Auto Smart Fix, in both Quick Fix and Full Edit modes.

The Red Eye Removal tool

For those stubborn red eye problems, the Red Eye Removal tool ( ) is a simple and efficient solution. You will now learn how to customize and use the tool to fix red eye in a photo.

1   Open the file 06_03.jpg in either Quick Fix or Full Edit mode.

2   In the toolbox, select the Red Eye Removal tool ( ).

3   In the tool options bar, do one of the following:

•   Click the Pupil Size menu, and then use the slider to set the value to about 25%.

•   Double-click the text box next to Pupil Size, and then type **25%**, followed by Return or Enter on your keyboard.

•   Hover the pointer over the Pupil Size text. When the pointer changes to the Scrubby slider icon ( ), click and drag to the left or right to select a Pupil Size of 25%.

4   With the Red Eye Removal tool selected, click and drag to select a rectangular area around one eye in the After image.

When you release the pointer, the red is removed from the eye. As an alternative to clicking and dragging to create a selection rectangle, you can click and release the pointer inside the red area of the eye.

5   With the Red Eye Removal tool still selected, click and release (don't drag!) the pointer inside the red area of the other eye.

The red is removed from the other eye.

6   (Optional) Click the Reset button, and then repeat steps 4 and 5 experimenting with other values for Pupil Size and Darken Amount in the tool options bar.

7   Choose File > Save As and navigate to the My CIB Work folder. Rename the file **06_03_Work** and select the JPEG format. If selected, deselect Save in Version Set with Original. Click Save, leaving all other options in the Save and JPEG Options dialog boxes unchanged.

8   Choose File > Close and return to the Organizer.

Making selections

Ordinarily, the entire image area can be altered by the changes you apply to an image or image layer. That's because, by default, the whole image is active. A selection is a portion of the image area that you designate as the only active area of the image. When a selection is active, any changes you apply affect only the area within the selection; the rest of the image layer is protected, or masked.

Typically, a selection marquee—a flashing border of dashed black and white lines—shows the boundaries of a selection. You can save a selection and re-use it at a later time. This can be a terrific time-saver when you need to use the selection several times.

Several tools create selections, and you'll get experience with most of them in the course of doing the lessons in this book. Selections can be geometric in shape or free form, and they can have crisp or soft edges. Selections can be created by using the mouse pointer, or by using similarities of color within the image.

Perhaps the simplest, most effective way to create a selection is to paint it on an image. This exercise focuses on the use of two selection tools in Photoshop Elements, the Selection Brush tool and the Quick Selection tool.

1   Using the Organizer, select the image of the water lily, 06_04.psd. Then, click the Editor button located near the top right corner of the Organizer window and choose Full Edit from the menu that appears. Or, use the keyboard shortcut Ctrl+I. Wait until the Editor has finished opening the file.

Notice that this file is saved as a Photoshop file and not as a JPEG file. The Photoshop file format can store additional information along with the image data. In this case, a portion of the flower has previously been selected and the selection information then saved in the file.

2   With the 06_04.psd file open in the Editor, choose Select > Load Selection. In the Load Selection dialog box, choose petals as Selection under Source. Under Operation, select New Selection, and then click OK. *(See illustration on the next page.)*

The selection information is loaded and becomes the current selection.

One petal needs to be added to make the selection of the flower complete. In the following exercise, you'll clear the current selection (the one you just loaded), use the Selection Brush tool to select just this one petal, and then reload the saved selection and add it to your new selection of the last missing petal.

3   Choose Select > Deselect to clear the current selection.

4   In the toolbox, select the Selection Brush tool (✐), which is grouped with the Quick Selection tool.

Using the Selection Brush tool

The Selection Brush tool makes selections in two ways. You can paint over the area you want to select in Selection mode, or you can paint over areas you don't want to select using a semi-opaque overlay in Mask mode.

1 From the tool options bar, set the Selection Brush controls to the following:

- Add to selection

- 25 pixels wide

- Mode: Selection

- Hardness: 100%

2 Click and drag with the Selection Brush to paint over the large interior area of the petal in the front. Do not try to paint the edges; you will do that in the next step.

Notice that as you paint, you're actually painting with the flashing dashed line that indicates a selection. Release the mouse button to see what you've selected.

💡 *To help in making the selection, you can use the Zoom tool to magnify the area of interest in the photo.*

Now you'll reduce your brush size and paint the edges of the petal, adding them to your selection as you paint.

While you could move the Size slider to change your brush size, it's easier to use the open bracket key ([ ) to size the brush down, and the close bracket key ( ]) to size the brush up. The brush size increases or decreases in size each time you press the open or close bracket keys.

3   Press the left bracket key ([ ), to reduce the Selection Brush size to 10 pixels.

4   With the Selection Brush, paint the edges of the petal by clicking and dragging over them.

> By switching the Mode in the tool options bar from Add to selection to Subtract from selection, you can use the Selection Brush to paint out the areas that you don't want selected or only accidentally selected in your image.

5   Continue to paint, using the brackets to change the brush size as needed, until the selection outline completely encompasses the petal.

If you found using the Selection Brush tool tedious, you'll appreciate learning about the Quick Selection tool later in this lesson. But first, you'll save the result of your hard work.

Editing a saved selection

Next you'll add your current selection to the selection that was saved with the file. You can modify saved selections by replacing, adding to, or subtracting from them.

1 With your selection still active, choose Select > Load Selection.

2 In the Load Selection dialog box, choose petals as Selection under Source. Choose Add to Selection under Operation, and then click OK.

Note: *The New Selection option replaces the saved selection with the current selection. Subtract from Selection subtracts the current selection from the saved selection. Intersect with Selection replaces the saved selection with the intersection between the current selection and the saved selection.*

You should now see the entire water lily outlined by the flashing selection boundary.

If you've missed a spot, simply paint it in with the Selection Brush tool. If you've selected too much, switch to Subtract from selection mode in the options bar, and then paint out your mistakes.

Note: *You can also modify a saved selection by loading it and using selection tools to add to it (Shift+drag) or subtract from it (Alt+drag).*

3   Choose Select > Save Selection. In the Save Selection dialog box, choose petals as Selection under Selection, select Replace Selection under Operation, and then click OK.

4   Choose Select > Deselect.

Using the Quick Selection Tool

The Quick Selection tool enables you to draw, scribble, or click on the area you want to select. The mark you make doesn't need to be precise, because while you are drawing, Photoshop Elements expands the selection border based on color and texture similarity.

For this exercise, you will first select the area around the water lily, and then swap the selected and unselected areas in the photo to establish the actual selection. This technique can be a real timesaver in situations where directly selecting an object proves difficult.

1   In the toolbox, select the Quick Selection tool ().

2   In the tool options bar, make sure New Selection is selected. Choose a brush size from the Size menu. If you want to simply scribble over the area, you can use a larger brush. For a more precise outline, choose a smaller brush size. For this exercise, you can use the default brush size of 30 px.

3   Scribble over the area around the water lily, making sure to touch some of the yellow, green and black areas as shown in the illustration, and then release the pointer. As you draw, Photoshop elements automatically expands the selection border based on color and texture similarity.

4   Continue to scribble over or click into unselected areas around the water lily until everything but the inside of the water lily is selected.

5   Finally, turn the selection inside out by choosing Select > Inverse, thereby masking the background and selecting the flower.

Working with selections

Now that you have a flashing selection outline around the water lily, you can change the color in the selected image area.

1 With the water lily still selected, click the Quick button at the top of the Edit panel of the Task pane to switch to Quick Fix mode.

2 To make comparing easier, choose Before & After - Horizontal from the View menu below the image to the left.

3 In the Color palette on the right, click and drag the Hue slider to the left or right to change the color of the water lily.

Notice that the water lily changes color, but the background does not. This is because only pixels inside the selection change.

4 Click the Cancel button (◎) in the Color palette to undo your changes.

You can invert the selection to apply changes to the background instead of the water lily.

5 Click the Full button at the top of the Edit panel to switch to Full Edit mode.

6 With the water lily still selected, choose Select > Inverse.

7 With the background around the water lily selected, choose Enhance > Convert to Black and White.

8	In the Convert to Black and White dialog box, choose Urban/Snapshots under Select a style.

9	(Optional) Select a different style to see the effect on the image. Use the sliders under Adjustment Intensity to vary the amount of change for red, green, blue, and contrast. Click Undo if you made changes you don't like.

10	Click OK to close the Convert to Black and White dialog box.

11	Choose Select > Deselect.

12	Choose File > Save As and save the file in the My CIB Work folder. For File Name, type **06_04_Work**. Make sure that the Format option is Photoshop (PSD). If Save in Version Set with Original is selected, deselect it before you click Save.

13	Choose File > Close, to close the file and switch back to the Organizer.

Congratulations, you've finished another exercise. In this exercise, you've learned how to use the Selection Brush tool and the Quick Selection tool to isolate areas of an image. You've also learned to mask out areas to which you don't want changes to be applied. And, you've learned how to add these new selections to existing, saved selections. This knowledge will be invaluable as you learn to use other selection tools.

Why won't Photoshop Elements do what I tell it to do?

In some situations, the changes you try to apply to an image may not seem to work. Or you may hear a beep sound, indicating that you're trying to do something that's not allowed. The following list offers explanations and solutions for common issues that might be blocking your progress.

Commit is required

Several tools, including the Type tool (T) require you to click the Commit button (✔) in the tool options bar before you can move on to another task. The same is true when you crop with the Crop tool or resize a layer or selection with the Move tool.

Cancel is required

The Undo command isn't available while you have uncommitted changes made with the Type tool, Move tool, or Crop tool, for example. If you want to undo such changes, click Cancel (◎) in the tool options bar instead of using the Undo command or shortcut.

Edits are restricted by an active selection

When you create a selection (using a marquee tool, the Quick Selection tool, or the Selection Brush tool, for example), you limit the active area of the image. Any edits you make will apply only within the selected area. If you try to make changes to an area outside the selection, nothing happens. If you want to deactivate a selection, choose Select > Deselect, and then you can work on any area of the image.

Edits are restricted by an active selection.

Move tool is required

If you drag a selection, the selection marquee moves, not the image within the selection marquee. If you want to move a selected part of the image or an entire layer, use the Move tool (▸⊕).

Background layer is selected

Many changes cannot be applied to the Background layer. For example, you can't erase, delete, change the opacity, or drag the Background layer to a higher level in the layer stack. If you need to apply changes to the Background layer, double-click it and rename it (or accept the default name, Layer 0).

Why won't Photoshop Elements do what I tell it to do? *(cont'd)*

Active layer is hidden

In most cases, the edits you make apply to only the currently selected layer—the one highlighted in the Layers palette. If an eye icon (👁) does not appear beside that layer in the Layers palette, then the layer is hidden and you cannot edit it. Or, if the image on the selected layer is not visible because it is blocked by an opaque upper layer, you will actually be changing that layer, but you won't see the changes in the image window.

The active layer is hidden, or layer view is blocked by opaque upper layer.

Active layer is locked

If you lock a layer by selecting the layer and then selecting the Lock (🔒) in the Layers palette, the lock prevents the layer from changing. To unlock a layer, select the layer, and then select the Lock at the top of the Layers palette to remove the Lock.

Active layer is locked.

Wrong layer is selected (for editing text)

If you want to make changes to a text layer, be sure that layer is selected in the Layers palette before you start. If a non-text layer is selected when you click the Type tool in the image window, Photoshop Elements creates a new text layer instead of placing the cursor in the existing text layer.

Replacing the color of a pictured object

Photoshop Elements offers two methods of swapping color, the Color Replacement tool and the Replace Color dialog box. With the Color Replacement tool (grouped in the toolbox with the Brush tool, the Impressionist Brush tool, and the Pencil tool) you can replace specific colors in your image by painting over a targeted color—for example, a yellow flower in an image—with a different color, like red. You can also use the Color Replacement tool to correct colors.

Using the Replace Color dialog box is faster and more automatic than using the Color Replacement tool, but it doesn't work well for all types of images. This method is easiest when the color of the object you want to change is not found in other areas of the image. The photograph of a yellow car used for this exercise has very little yellow elsewhere in the image, making it a good example for this approach.

Replacing a color throughout the image

In this project, you'll change the color of a yellow car. You'll do your work on a duplicate of the Background layer, which later makes it easy to compare the finished project with the original picture.

What's nice about the Replace Color feature is that you don't have to be too meticulous when you apply it, while still producing spectacular results. You're going to do this exercise twice. First, you'll work on the entire image area. This will show you how much the color changes will affect the areas outside the car, such as the trees in the background. You will then use an area selection for the second part of this exercise.

1   Using the Organizer, find the file 06_05.psd, the picture of the yellow car, and then open it in the Editor in Full Edit mode.

2   In the Editor, choose Layer > Duplicate Layer and accept the default name. Alternatively, drag the Background layer up to the New Layer icon (◻) in the Layers palette. By duplicating the layer, you have an original to return to if you need it.

3   With the Background copy layer still selected in the Layers palette, choose Enhance > Adjust Color > Replace Color.

4   In the Replace Color dialog box, select Image under Selection so that you see the color thumbnail of the car picture. Make sure that the Eyedropper tool (🖉) within the dialog box is selected. Then, click the yellow paint area of the car.

5   Click the Selection option under the thumbnail image to see the selection, or color-application area, indicated as white on a black background.

6   Drag the Hue slider, and optionally the Saturation and Lightness slider to change the color of the selected area. For example, try Hue = −88 to change the yellow to pink.

7 To adjust the color-application area, start by selecting the Add to Sample eyedropper (🖉), and then click in the edit window in areas where the paint on the car still appears yellow.

8 Drag the Fuzziness slider left or right until you find an acceptable compromise between the color replacement on the car and the effect on other image areas.

9 When you are satisfied with the results, click OK to close the Replace Color dialog box.

Depending on what color and color characteristics you used to replace the yellow, you probably can see a shift in the color of the trees in the background. If this is a compromise you can live with, that's great. If not, you may need to try another technique. This is what you'll do in the next procedure.

Replacing a color in a limited area of the image

You're going to try the previous procedure again, but this time you'll limit the color change to a selected image area.

1 Choose Edit > Undo Replace Color, or select the step before Replace Color in the Undo History palette (Window > Undo History).

2 In the toolbox, select the Lasso tool (𝒫) and click and drag with the pointer to draw a rough selection around the car. It's OK if some of the road and the wall in the background are included in the selection.

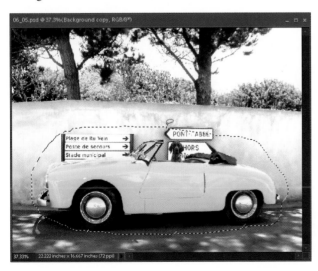

Note: The Lasso tool is grouped with the Magnetic Lasso tool and the Polygonal Lasso tool in the toolbox. To switch from one lasso tool to another, click the tool in the toolbox and keep the pointer pressed until a menu appears, and then choose the other tool from the menu.

3   In the tool options bar, select Subtract from selection ( ), and then drag a shape around the yellow sticker on the windshield to remove it from the selection.

Note: Zooming in for this part of the process may be helpful. Use the slider in the Navigator palette (Window > Navigator) to zoom in so that you don't have to switch tools, or use the zoom-in keyboard shortcut, Ctrl+ = (equal sign).

4   Choose Enhance > Adjust Color > Replace Color.

5   Using the same techniques and settings you used in the previous procedure, make adjustments in the Replace Color dialog box to change the color of the car. (See "Replacing a color throughout the image," steps 4-8.)

6   When you are satisfied with the results, click OK to close the dialog box.

7   Choose Select > Deselect, or press Ctrl+D.

8   Choose File > Save As and save the file in the My CIB Work folder. For File Name, type **06_05_Work**. Make sure that the Format option is Photoshop (PSD). If Save in Version Set with Original is selected, deselect it before you click Save.

9   Choose File > Close, to close the file and return to the Organizer.

Take a bow—you've finished the five exercises in this lesson. In the last exercise, you learned how to make a selection with the Lasso tool and how to edit that selection to make it fit more closely. You then replaced one color with another using the Replace Color dialog box. In the process, you've also used the Undo History palette to step backwards to a specific point in your work.

About printing color pictures

Sometimes, pictures that look great on your computer don't turn out so well when you print them. How can you make them look as good in print as they do on screen?

Color problems can arise from a variety of sources. One may be the camera or the conditions under which a photograph was taken. If a photograph is flawed, you can usually make it better by editing it with Photoshop Elements, as you did with the images in this lesson.

There are other possible contributors to color problems. One may be your monitor, which may shift colors. You can correct that by calibrating your monitor.

Another possibility is that your color printer interprets color information differently than your computer. You can correct that by activating the appropriate type of color management.

Working with color management

Moving an image from your camera to your monitor and from there to a printer makes the image colors shift. This shift occurs because every device has a different color gamut, or range of colors that it can generate. To achieve consistent color between digital cameras, scanners, computer monitors, and printers, you need to use color management.

Color management software acts as a color interpreter, translating the image colors so that each device can reproduce them in the same way. This software knows how each device and program understands color, and adjusts colors so that those you see on your monitor are similar to the colors in your printed image. It should be noted, however, that not all colors may match exactly.

Color management is achieved through the use of profiles, or mathematical descriptions of each device's color space. If these profiles are compliant with the standards of the ICC (International Color Consortium), they help you maintain consistent color.

Photoshop Elements' color management controls are located under the Edit menu.

Setting up color management

1   In the Editor, choose Edit > Color Settings.

2   Select one of these color management options:

•   **No Color Management** uses your monitor profile as the working space. It removes any embedded profiles when opening images, and does not apply a profile when saving.

•   **Always Optimize Colors for Computer Screens** uses sRGB as the working space, preserves embedded profiles, and assigns sRGB when opening untagged files.

•   **Always Optimize for Printing** uses Adobe RGB as the working space, preserves embedded profiles, and assigns Adobe RGB when opening untagged files.

•   **Allow Me to Choose** lets you choose to assign sRGB (the default) or Adobe RGB when opening untagged files.

3   Click OK to close the Color Settings dialog box.

Note: When you save a file, select ICC Profile in the Save As dialog box.

Further information on color management, including monitor calibration, can be found in a series of topics in Help. To access this information, choose Help > Photoshop Elements Help and search for these subjects.

Review

▶ ## Review questions

1   What is the key difference between adjusting images in Full Edit mode, Quick Fix mode, or Guided Edit mode?

2   Can you apply automatic fixes when you are in Full Edit mode?

3   What tools can you use to fix the red-eye phenomenon created by some flash cameras?

4   What makes selections so important for adjusting color?

5   Name at least two selection tools and describe how they work.

Review answers

1   Full Edit provides a more flexible and powerful image correction environment. Full Edit has lighting and color correction commands, along with tools you'll need to fix image defects, make selections, add text, and paint on your images. Quick Fix provides access to the more basic photo fixing controls in Photoshop Elements, and enables you to make quick adjustments to your images using those controls. If you are new to digital photography, Guided Edit is the place to start for fixing common image problems. Edit capabilities are restricted or simplified. Guided Edit also offers guided activities taking you step-by-step through several image editing tasks to get professional results.

2   Yes. The Enhance menu contains commands that are equivalent to the buttons in the Quick Fix palettes: Auto Smart Fix, Auto Levels, Auto Contrast, Auto Color Correction, and Auto Red Eye Fix. The Enhance menu also provides an Adjust Smart Fix command, which opens a dialog box in which you can change the amount of automatic fixing.

3   You can choose to automatically fix red eye when importing photos into the catalog. Simply select Automatically Fix Red Eye where available in the various import dialog boxes. To fix red eye after the photos have been imported, choose Edit > Auto Red Eye Fix in the Organizer. In either the Full Edit or Quick Fix mode of the Editor, choose Enhance > Auto Red Eye Fix. Finally, the Red Eye

Removal tool located in the toolbox enables you to adjust some parameters while fixing red eye.

4 You use a selection to define an area as the only part of a layer that can be altered. The areas outside the selection are protected from change for as long as the selection is active. This aids greatly in image correction, as it enables you make different adjustments to selected portions of your image.

5 The first tool you used in this lesson to make selections is the Selection Brush tool, which works like a paintbrush. The Quick Selection tool is similar to the Selection Brush tool, but in most cases a faster, more flexible option for creating a selection. The Lasso tool creates free-form selections; you drag the Lasso tool around the area that you want to select. There are even more tools than discussed in this lesson to create selections. The Magic Wand tool selects all the areas with the same color as the color on which you click. The Rectangular Marquee tool and the Elliptical Marquee tool make selections in fixed geometric shapes when you drag them across the image. The Magnetic Lasso tool helps to draw selections along the (possibly quite irregular) edge of an object while the Polygonal Lasso tool restricts drawing to straight lines, making it the tool of choice to select regular shaped objects.

7 | Fixing Exposure Problems

You can use Photoshop Elements to fix many images that are too dark or too light and rescue some pictures that you perceive as being terribly awful, hopelessly bad, useless, and not very good either. The Automatic and Quick Fix modes with their limited options might be all you ever need to accomplish those goals. However, depending of the image, there are more sophisticated methods for even better results.

This lesson leads you through several approaches to correcting exposure problems in photographs. This aspect of image correction is often easier to deal with than you might imagine.

In this lesson, you will learn how to do the following:

- Brighten underexposed photographs.
- Correct different areas of an image individually.
- Save selection shapes to reuse in later sessions.
- Create and apply adjustment layers.
- Bring out details and colors in overexposed and faded photographs.

This lesson assumes that you are already familiar with the overall features of the Photoshop Elements work area, and recognize the two ways in which you can use Photoshop Elements: the Editor and the Organizer. If you need to learn more about these items, see Lesson 1, "A Quick Tour of Photoshop Elements" and Photoshop Elements Help. This lesson also builds on the skills and concepts covered in the earlier lessons.

Before you begin, make sure that you have correctly copied the Lessons folder from the CD in the back of this book onto your computer's hard disk. See "Copying the Classroom in a Book files" on page 3.

Getting started

While working on the projects in this lesson, you'll use the CIB Catalog you created in the "Getting Started" section at the beginning of this book. To use the CIB Catalog, follow these steps:

1   Start Photoshop Elements. In the Welcome Screen, click Organize in the row of shortcut buttons across the lower part of the Welcome Screen. If the CIB Catalog is open, skip to the next section, "Correcting images automatically as batch process." If the CIB Catalog is not open, complete the following steps.

2   Choose File > Catalog.

3   In the Catalog Manager dialog box, select the CIB Catalog under Catalogs, and then click Open.

If you do not see the CIB Catalog file, review the procedures found in "Getting Started." See "Copying the Lessons files from the CD" on page 3, and "Creating a catalog" on page 4.

Correcting images automatically as batch process

You'll start this lesson in the same way that you began your work in Lesson 6. You will process all the image files for this lesson in one session to apply automatic fixes available in Photoshop Elements. You'll save these files so that you can compare them to the files that you fix using manual techniques.

1   Start Photoshop Elements in Full Edit mode by clicking Edit in the Welcome Screen. Or, if the Organizer is already open, click the Editor button () located near the top right corner of the Organizer window, and then choose Full Edit from the menu.

2   If the Editor is already open from an earlier exercise, switch to Full Edit mode if necessary, by clicking the Full tab in the Edit pane of the Task panel.

3 Choose File > Process Multiple Files.

4 In the Process Multiple Files dialog box, do the following:

• Choose Folder from the Process Files From menu.

• Under Source, click Browse. Find and select the Lesson07 folder in the Lessons folder. Click OK to close the Browse for Folder dialog box.

• Under Destination, click Browse. Find and select the My CIB Work folder that you created at the start of the book. Click OK to close the Browse for Folder dialog box.

5 Under File Naming, select Rename Files. Select Document Name in the first field, and type **_Autofix** in the second field. This adds the appendix "_Autofix" to the existing document name as the files are saved in the My CIB Work folder.

6 Under Quick Fix on the right side of the dialog box, select all four options: Auto Levels, Auto Contrast, Auto Color, and Sharpen.

7 Review all selections in the dialog box, comparing them to the following illustration. Make sure that the Resize Images and the Convert Files to options are not selected. Then, click OK.

Photoshop Elements takes a few seconds to process the files. Image windows will open and close automatically as the adjustments are applied. There's nothing else you need to do. If any alerts or warnings are displayed, click OK.

At the end of this lesson, you can compare the results of this simple, automatic fixing of the images with the results from applying the manual techniques in the exercises. In many cases, the automatic method of fixing files may be sufficient to meet your needs.

Brightening an underexposed image

Slightly underexposed photographs look dingy and dull. While the auto-fix lighting feature does a terrific job of brightening up many of these photos, here you'll use different methods to adjust the exposure.

Applying the Quick Fix

1   If the Organizer is not currently active, switch to it now.

2   In the Keyword Tags palette, click the Find box next to the Lesson 7 keyword tag.

3   Click to select the file 07_01.jpg, a badly underexposed image of a woman in the countryside.

Note: To show the file names in the Photo Browser, choose View > Show File Names.

4   Click the Editor button (📝) located near the top right corner of the Organizer window, and then choose Quick Fix from the menu.

Photoshop Elements will load the Editor workspace and open the image in Quick Fix mode.

5   Under General Fixes, click the Auto button next to Smart Fix. *(See illustration on the next page.)* Notice how the dark areas in the picture become brighter.

6   Under Lighting, make the following adjustments:

• Drag the Lighten Shadows to the right by one grey measuring bar.

• Drag the Darken Highlights slider just slightly to the right.

Of course, you can experiment with those sliders to see the range of changes you might apply to an image.

7   Click the Commit button (✔) in the Lighting palette title bar to commit the changes.

8   Choose File > Save As. In the Save As dialog box, navigate to and open the My CIB Work folder, rename the file **07_01_Quick** and select the JPEG format. If Save in Version Set with Original is selected, deselect it. Click Save. In the JPEG Options dialog box, select High from the Quality menu, and then click OK

9   Choose File > Close and return to the Organizer.

Without much effort the image has improved significantly. You'll now use other methods to adjust the lighting in the image and compare the results later on.

Employing Guided Edit

1   With the image 07_01.jpg still selected in the Photo Browser of the Organizer, click the Editor button, and then choose Guided Edit from the menu that appears. The Editor workspace will load and open the same underexposed, original photo you used in the previous exercise, but this time in Guided Edit mode.

2   If necessary, click the triangle next to Lighting and Exposure under What would you like to do. Then, click to select Lighten or Darken. This opens the Lighten or Darken a Photo panel with its different options.

3   Click the Auto button near the top right corner of the Lighten or Darken a Photo panel. Notice that in this case the result is not quite as good as you would expect. Click the Undo button above the Edit pane, or choose Edit > Undo Auto Levels to revert the image to its original state.

4   Use the sliders to manually adjust the lighting in the image. Drag the Lighten Shadows slider to a value of 30, the Darken Highlights slider to a value of 55, and the Midtone Contrasts to a value of 25. Then, click Done.

💡 *If you want to return to the original settings and start from scratch, click the Reset button.*

5   Choose File > Save As. In the Save As dialog box, navigate to and open the My CIB Work folder, rename the file **07_01_Guided** and select the JPEG format. If Save in Version Set with Original is selected, deselect it. Click Save. In the JPEG Options dialog box, select High from the Quality menu, and then click OK.

6   Choose File > Close and return to the Organizer.

Again, the image now looks considerably better than its original. However, it would be ideal if the woman and the foreground were treated differently than the background with the landscape and sky.

Fixing an image in Full Edit mode

If your photo is suffering from excessive backlighting, as is the case with our example, more elaborate methods might be necessary to achieve better results. Increasing the number of layers and applying blending modes, as well as isolating parts of the image and treating them independently, are possible in the Full Edit mode.

Adding Blending modes

To use blending modes, you need to have two or more layers. The layer mode applied to a layer can be used to affect the appearance of the image in the layer below it. As an example, if your photo is too dark, adding a duplicated layer on top and selecting Screen as layer mode might correct the problem. On the other hand, if your photo is too light, duplicating the photo layer and choosing Multiply as layer mode might be the solution.

1   With the image 07_01.jpg still selected in the Photo Browser of the Organizer, click the Editor button, and then choose Full Edit from the menu that appears. The Editor workspace will load and open the image in Full Edit mode.

2   Do only one of the following to duplicate the Background layer of the image:

• With the Background layer selected in the Layers palette, choose Layer > Duplicate Layer, and then click OK in the Duplicate Layer dialog box, accepting the default name.

• Right-click the Background layer in the Layers palette and choose Duplicate Layer from the context menu. Click OK in the Duplicate Layer dialog box, accepting the default name.

• Drag and drop the Background layer on the New Layer button (▣) in the Layers palette.

The new Background copy layer is highlighted in the Layers palette, indicating that it is the selected (active) layer.

3   With the Background copy layer selected in the Layers palette, choose Screen from the layer blending mode menu. Notice how the image becomes brighter.

Note: If the layer blending mode menu is disabled, make sure that the Background copy layer, not the original Background layer, is selected in the Layers palette.

4   Choose File > Save As.

5   In the Save As dialog box, name the file **07_01_Screen** and save it in the My CIB Work folder, with Photoshop (PSD) as Format and the Layers option selected. If Save in Version Set with Original is selected, deselect it before you click Save. If the Photoshop Elements Format Options dialog box appears, keep Maximize Compatibility selected and click OK.

6   Toggle the visibility of the Background copy layer in the Layers palette to compare the original with the final image. When you've finished comparing, close the file without saving and return to the Organizer.

Here you've seen how blending modes can brighten up a dull image. However, one needs to be careful with applying blending modes over the entire image, as often it can ruin the exposure of parts of the photos that were OK to begin with. In this example, almost all details of the sky have been lost. Using layers, there are ways to obtain even better results. In the following exercises, you'll use other blending modes to correct different kinds of image problems.

Adjusting color curves

Using the Adjust Color Curves command is a great way for quickly fixing some exposure problems. You can improve color tones in a photo by adjusting highlights, midtones, and shadows in each color channel. For example, this command can fix photos with darkened images due to strong backlighting, or those that appear washed out due to harsh lighting.

In the Adjust Color Curves dialog box, you compare and choose different tonal presets represented by image thumbnails. To fine-tune the adjustment, display Advanced Options section and adjust highlights, midtone brightness and contrast, and shadows.

To preserve the original photo while experimenting, make the color curve adjustments on a duplicate layer.

—From Photoshop Elements Help

To open the Adjust Color Curves dialog box, choose Enhance > Adjust Color > Adjust Color Curves. To adjust only a specific area of the image, select it with one of the selection tools before opening the dialog box.

For of our sample image, first selecting the Lighten Shadows style preset, and then manually adjusting the highlights and shadows seems to work best.

Using adjustment layers

Sometimes you need to go back and tweak your settings after the first adjustment, or even during a much later work session. Compared to image layers, adjustment layers (and fill layers) are special types of layers.

An adjustment layer is like a colored veil on top of your underlying layers. Any changes applied on an adjustment layer can be easily revised, because the pixels of the image are not permanently modified. This is an appreciable advantage, especially when you wish to apply the same changes to several images. You can either copy the adjustment layer and place it on top of the other photo, or use the Process Multiple files command (for more information please refer to Photoshop Elements Help).

Creating adjustment layers for lighting

In this next activity, we'll continue to use the same underexposed photograph to explore improving the image through the addition of an adjustment layer.

1   With the image 07_01.jpg still selected in the Photo Browser of the Organizer, click the Editor button, and then choose Full Edit from the menu that appears.

2   With the Background layer selected in the Layers palette, click the Create Adjustment Layer button (⊘.) and choose Brightness/Contrast from the menu that appears.

3   If necessary, drag the Brightness/Contrast dialog box aside so that you can also see most of the image window. Make sure the Preview box is checked. In the Brightness/Contrast dialog box, drag the sliders so that Brightness is +50 and Contrast is +10, and then click OK. *(See illustration on the next page.)*

4   Click the Create Adjustment Layer button again, but this time choose Levels (instead of Brightness/Contrast) from the menu. Levels is an effective tonal and color adjustment tool. Notice the additional layer created in the Layers palette.

5   In the Levels dialog box, drag the black, white, and gray arrows (assigned for the shadow values, middle tones and highlight values respectively) that are under the graph to the left or right until the balance of dark and light areas looks right to you. We selected values of 20, 2.0, and 190.

6   Click OK to close the Levels dialog box. The overall improvements to the image are similar to those made in Quick Fix mode.

7   Choose File > Save As. In the Save As dialog box, name the file **07_01_Adjustment** and save it in the My CIB Work folder, with Photoshop (PSD) as Format and the Layers option selected. If Save in Version Set with Original is selected, deselect it before you click Save. If the Photoshop Elements Format Options dialog box appears, keep Maximize Compatibility selected and click OK.

8   Close the file and return to the Organizer.

The beauty of adjustment layers is that you can revert to earlier settings, even in later work sessions, as long as you save the file in the Photoshop (PSD) format, preserving the layers (the default). For example, if you reopen your file and double-click the Brightness/Contrast icon in the layer thumbnail, your original settings (+50 and +10) still appear in the Brightness/Contrast dialog box, and can be further refined.

If necessary, you can even revert to the original, uncorrected image by either hiding or deleting the adjustment layers.

Correcting parts of an image

Although the adjustment layers do a fine job of bringing out the colors and details from the dark original image, the background is now too washed out. When you made corrections to the image earlier in this lesson, they applied to the entire picture. Now you will restrict the adjustments to sections of the image.

Creating a selection

In this task, you'll divide the picture into two parts: the woman in the foreground, and the background with the landscape and sky. You'll start out by selecting the silhouette of the woman in order to place it on a separate layer. This layer can then be adjusted separately from the background layer.

There are different ways of making a selection. You already used some of them in Lesson 6. The choice of tools depends largely on the picture. For our purposes here, we'll start by using the Quick Selection tool, which makes a selection based on texture similarity. By merrily scribbling inside an object the Quick Selection tool automatically determines the selection borders for you, as you will see in the following exercise.

1   With the image 07_01.jpg still selected in the Photo Browser of the Organizer, click the Editor button, and then choose Full Edit from the menu that appears.

2   In the toolbox, select the Quick Selection tool (✎), which is grouped with the Selection Brush tool.

3   Make sure New selection is selected in the tool options bar.

4   Place the cursor at the lower center of the woman and slowly drag a line to the top of her head. Notice as you proceed how the active selection automatically expands to create a border around the silhouette of the woman. Not bad at all for a quick selection!

Next you need to refine the border a little to capture the silhouette as closely as possible. You want to deselect the triangle under the arm on the left and tighten the selection along the neck and the other arm. For this you use the Add to Selection tool (✎) and the Subtract from selection tool (✎), located next to the New selection button.

5   Select Subtract from selection (✎) in the options bar in order to prepare for taking away parts from the selection.

6   Draw a line over selected areas of the image background and you will see the flashing selection outline receding toward the silhouette. Reduce the Brush size as necessary—by pressing the '[' key on your keyboard—to make finer adjustments. Use the Zoom tool to zoom into the image.

7   Repeat these steps using the Add to Selection tool (✎) and the Subtract from selection tool (✎) to tighten up the selection. You should end up with a tight flashing selection outline around the silhouette of the woman in the foreground.

8   To soften the hard edges of the selection, you will smooth and feather the outline. Click Refine Edge in the tool options bar.

9   In the Refine Edge dialog box, enter **8** for Smooth and **4** pixels for the Feather, and then click OK. You can select the Zoom tool as well as the Hand tool from within the dialog box to get a better view of the details of your selection.

10   Choose Select > Save Selection. In the Save Selection dialog box, choose New from the Selection menu and type **Woman** to name the selection. Then, click OK. Saving a selection is always a good idea, because it facilitates its re-use at a later time.

Correcting overexposed areas

One of the aims in this exercise is to intensify the color and contrast in the overexposed area of the trees and sky. The woman in the foreground is already a bit darker, so you won't want to intensify this area. Your approach here is to divide and conquer—to apply different solutions to different areas of the image. Creating a copy of just the area you selected is the first step in this process. To make the job easier, let's make sure that the thumbnails are of a satisfactory size.

1 Choose Palette Options from the Layers palette menu.

2 In the Layers Palette Options dialog box, select the medium sized thumbnail option, if it is not already selected, and then click OK.

Selecting another size is OK, but do not select None. The layer thumbnail can help you visualize the layers you will work with in this project.

3 With the Zoom tool selected in the toolbox, click Fit Screen in the tool options bar so that you can see the entire image.

4   Do one of the following:

•   If the selection you made in the previous topic is still active, choose Select > Inverse, and then go to Step 5.

•   If the selection is not active, choose Select > Load Selection. Under Source, select Woman from the Selection menu and select the Invert option. Make sure New Selection is selected under Operation, and then click OK.

5   Choose Edit > Copy to copy the selected area.

6   Choose Edit > Paste to paste the copied area onto a new layer, Layer 1.

In the image window, the only difference you'll see is that the selection marquee has disappeared. But in the Layers palette you can see that there's a new layer.

7   In the Layers palette, select the Background layer. Choose Select > Load Selection. Under Source, select Woman from the Selection menu, but this time do not select the Invert option. Then, click OK.

8   Choose Edit > Copy.

9   With the Background layer selected in the Layers palette, choose Edit > Paste. Now you've got three layers on top of each other: Layer 1 with the landscape and sky, Layer 2 featuring the silhouette of the woman, and the Background layer with the entire photo.

10 Especially when working with multiple layers, life is made easier when you name layers descriptively. To do this, double-click the name of the layer. The pointer changes to the Type tool and a text box to type into appears. Type **Landscape** for Layer 1 and **Woman** for Layer 2.

Now you can start to work on those layers individually to improve the overall photo.

Correcting underexposed areas

You can lighten the shadows of just the underexposed areas using the same techniques you used earlier on the entire image.

1 In the Layers palette, click the Woman layer to select it, and then choose Screen as the blending mode. Notice that the entire silhouette is now brighter and the details are more discernable, while the Landscape layer with the undergrowth stays exactly as before.

2 (Optional) Choose Enhance > Auto Sharpen.

Adding more intensity

Now that the foreground looks better, the background needs to be adjusted to appear less washed out.

1 In the Layers palette, select the Landscape layer.

2 Choose Darker Color as blending mode and notice how the background shows more detail with some clouds appearing in the sky.

3 (Optional) To further improve the appearance of the sky, copy just the sky area from the Background image into a new layer on top of the other layers. Then, change the blending mode to Multiply.

With these few adjustment to the different layers, the entire photograph now looks much more lively. There are still a lot of possibilities to continue playing around with the brightness and intensities in different areas, as well as the opacities of the layers—you will learn those techniques later in this lesson. However, this exercise has been a good start towards understanding the basic principles of separating an image into selections on different layers, and working with those layers individually.

4 When you are satisfied with the results, choose File > Save As.

5 In the Save As dialog box, name the file **07_01_Layers** and save it in the My CIB Work folder, with Photoshop (PSD) as Format and the Layers option selected. If Save in Version Set with Original is selected, deselect it before you click Save. If the Photoshop

Elements Format Options dialog box appears, keep Maximize Compatibility selected and click OK.

6 Close the file and return to the Organizer.

In Lesson 6 you learned how you can arrange the windows to best compare your results from your different methods of adjusting the image. Using this technique you might want to compare the results from working on this image before going to the next project.

Improving faded or overexposed images

In this exercise, you'll work with the scan of an old photograph that has faded badly and is in danger of being lost forever. Although it's not necessarily an award-winning shot, it could represent a treasured aspect of personal history, like our example of a beloved grandmother and her twin sister when they were babies, which you might want to preserve for future generations.

The automatic fixes you applied to a copy of this image at the beginning of this lesson (See "Correcting images automatically as batch process") improve the photograph quite a bit. In this project, you'll try to do even better using other techniques.

Creating a set of duplicate files

You're going to compare a variety of techniques during the course of this project. You'll start by creating individual files for each technique and giving them unique names. These names will help you identify the technique used to adjust each file.

1   If the Organizer is not currently active, switch to it now.

2   In the Keyword Tags palette, click the Find box next to the Lesson 7 keyword tag.

3   Click to select the file 07_02.jpg, a faded picture of the baby twins.

4   With the image 07_02.jpg selected in the Photo Browser of the Organizer, click the Editor button (🖉) located near the top right corner of the Organizer window, and then choose Full Edit from the menu that appears.

The Editor workspace will load and open the image in Full Edit mode.

5   In the Editor, choose File > Duplicate. In the Duplicate Image dialog box, type **07_02_Shad_High**, and then click OK.

6   Repeat Step 5 two more times, naming the duplicate files **07_02_Bright_Con** and **07_02_Levels**.

7   In the Project Bin, double-click the 07_02.jpg thumbnail to make that image active. You can see the file names in a tool tip window when you hover the pointer over the thumbnail images in the Project Bin.

8   Choose File > Save As. When a dialog box appears, type **07_02_Blend_Mode** as the new file name and select Photoshop (PSD) in the Format menu. Select the My CIB Work folder as the Save In location. If Save in Version Set with Original is selected, deselect it before you click Save. Click OK in any dialog boxes or messages that appear, to accept the default settings. Leave all four images open for the rest of the project.

9   Choose Window > Images > Tile.

Using blending modes to fix a faded image

This technique is similar to the one you used earlier to correct an underexposed image. In this case, you'll use other blending modes to fix the exposure.

Blending modes make layers interact with the layers under them in various ways. Multiply intensifies the dark pixels in an image. Overlay tends to brighten an image. For this project, using Overlay adds clarity and brilliance without canceling out the effect of the Multiply blending mode on the underlying layers.

The stacking order of the layers makes a difference, so if you dragged one of the Multiply blending mode layers to the top of the layer stack, you'd see slightly different results.

1   Make sure that the 07_02_Blend_Mode.psd file is the active window. If necessary, double-click its thumbnail in the Project Bin to make it active.

2   Duplicate the Background layer by choosing Layer > Duplicate Layer. Click OK in the Duplicate Layer dialog box, accepting the default name, Background copy.
Leave the Background copy layer selected in the Layers palette for the next step.

3   In the Layers palette, do the following:

• Choose Multiply from the layer blending mode menu.

• Drag and drop the Background copy layer onto the New Layer icon () to create a copy of the Background copy layer, named Background copy 2.

4   In the Layers palette, select the following options for the Background copy 2 layer:

• Change the layer blending mode from Multiply to Overlay.

• Set the Opacity to 50%, either by entering the value in the text field or by dragging the Opacity slider.

The Overlay blending mode brightens the image considerably, but the image contrast is still unimpressive.

5   (Optional) Fine-tune the results by adjusting the Opacity settings for the two background copy layers until you achieve a pleasing balance.

Note: You cannot change the Opacity of the locked Background layer.

6   Choose File > Save to save the file in the My CIB Work folder. Leave the file open.

7   If a message appears about maximizing compatibility, click OK to close it. Or, follow the instructions in the message to prevent it from appearing again.

Adjusting shadows and highlights manually

Although both auto-fixing and blending modes do a good job of correcting fading images, some of your own photos may be more challenging. You'll try three new techniques in the next three procedures.

The first technique involves making adjustments for Shadows, Highlights, and Midtone Contrast.

1   In the Project Bin, double-click the 07_02_Shad_High thumbnail image to make it the active window.

2   Choose Enhance > Adjust Lighting > Shadows/Highlights.

3   Select the Preview option in the Shadows/Highlights dialog box, if it is not already selected. If necessary, move the dialog box so that you can also see most of the 07_02_Shad_High image window.

By default, the Lighten Shadows setting is 25%, so you'll see a difference in the image already.

4   In the Shadows/Highlights dialog box, do all the following:

- Drag the Lighten Shadows slider to 30%, or type **30**.

- Drag the Darken Highlights slider to 15%, or type **15**.

- Drag the Midtone Contrast slider to about +20%, or type **20**.

5   (Optional) Adjust the three settings as needed until you think the image is as good as it can be.

6 When done, click OK to close the Shadows/Highlights dialog box.

7 Choose File > Save As and save the file as 07_02_Shad_High in the My CIB Work folder, selecting JPEG as format. Click OK to accept the default settings in the JPEG Options dialog box. Leave the file open.

💡 *The adjustments you used in this technique are also available in the Lighting palette in Quick Fix mode.*

Adjusting brightness and contrast manually

The next approach you'll take for fixing exposure problems uses another dialog box, which is also available from the Enhance > Adjust Lighting menu.

1 In the Project Bin, double-click the 07_02_Bright_Con thumbnail to make it active.

2 Choose Enhance > Adjust Lighting > Brightness/Contrast.
If necessary, drag the Brightness/Contrast dialog box aside so that you can also see most of the 07_02_Bright_Con image window.

3 In the Brightness/Contrast dialog box, do all the following:

• Select Preview, if it is not already selected.

• Drag the Brightness slider to -20, or type **-20** in the text field, being careful to include the minus sign when you type. *(See illustration on the next page.)*

- Drag to set the Contrast at +40, or type **+40** in the text field.

4 (Optional) Adjust the Brightness and Contrast settings until you are happy with the quality of the image.

5 Click OK to close the Brightness/Contrast dialog box.

6 Choose File > Save As and save the file as 07_02_Bright_Con in the My CIB Work folder, selecting JPEG as format. Click OK when the JPEG Options dialog box appears. Leave the file open.

Adjusting levels

Levels are the range of color values—the degree of darkness or lightness, whether the color is red, yellow, purple, or another color. In this procedure, you'll enhance the photograph by shifting the reference points for levels.

1 In the Project Bin, double-click the 07_02_Levels thumbnail image to make it the active window.

2 Choose Enhance > Adjust Lighting > Levels.

3 Select the Preview option in the Levels dialog box, if it is not already selected.

The graph represents the distribution of pixel values in the image. In this image there are no truly white pixels or truly black pixels. By dragging the sliders inward to where the pixels start to appear in the graph, you redefine what levels are calculated as dark and light. This enhances the contrast between the lightest pixels in the image and the darkest ones.

If necessary, drag the dialog box aside so that you can also see most of the image window.

4   In the Levels dialog box, do all of the following:

•   Drag the black triangle that is beneath the left side of the graph to the right and position it under the first steep spike in the graph shape. At that position, the value in the first Input Levels box is approximately 42.

•   Drag the white triangle on the right side of the graph until it reaches the edge of the final spike in the graph shape. The value of the third Input Levels box changes to approximately 225.

•   Drag the gray center triangle under the graph toward the right until the middle Input Level value is approximately 0.90. Click OK to close the Levels dialog box.

5   Choose File > Save As and save the file as 07_02_Levels in the My CIB Work folder, selecting JPEG as format. Click OK to accept the default settings in the JPEG Options dialog box. Leave the file open.

Comparing results

You can now compare the six versions of the image: the original file, these four files you have just prepared, and the one file that you auto-fixed in a batch process at the beginning of this lesson.

1　In Full Edit, choose File > Open, and then find and open the file 07_02_ Autofix.jpg in the My CIB Work folder. If you can't see the file in the Open dialog box, make sure All Formats is selected in the Files of type menu.

2　Choose File > Open, and then find and open the file 07_02.jpg in the Lesson 7 folder. If you can't see the file in the Open dialog box, make sure All Formats is selected in the Files of type menu.

3　In the Project Bin, make sure that only the six files for this project are open: 07_ 02_Blend_Mode.psd, 07_02_Shad_High.jpg, 07_02_Bright_Con.jpg, 07_02_Levels.jpg, 07_02_Autofix.jpg, and the original 07_02.jpg. Make sure, no other files are open. To see the file names displayed under the thumbnails in the Project Bin, right-click an empty area in the Project Bin, and then select Show Filenames.

4　Choose Window > Images > Tile, if it is not already selected.

5　Now you'll reduce the zoom level for all active windows. Select the Zoom tool (🔍). In the tool options bar, select Zoom Out and Zoom All Windows. Then, click in any image window until you can see a large enough image area to be able to compare the different results. Or, zoom in to focus on a detail. Select the area of interest in one window, and then choose Window > Images > Match Zoom and Windows > Images > Match Location.

6 Compare the results and pick your favorite. The best method for fixing a file depends on the type of problem being addressed, the affected areas of the image, and how you will use the resulting image.

7 Click Window > Images > Tile again to deselect it. You won't see any difference in the arrangement of image windows, but it will stop the automatic rearrangement when you open or close other images.

8 Choose File > Close All. Save your changes if prompted to do so in My CIB Work folder and return to the Organizer.

Congratulations! You've now finished Lesson 7. In doing so, you've used various automatic and manual approaches to correct overexposed photographs and scans of faded prints. You've tried auto-fixes, blending modes, and the three dialog boxes that are available under the Enhance > Adjust Lighting menu. You know that you can apply these different adjustments either in layers, on selections, separately, or in combinations.

Review

▶ **Review questions**

1 Describe two ways to create an exact copy of an existing layer.

2 Where can you find the controls for adjusting the lighting in a photograph?

3 How do you change the arrangement of image windows in the work area?

4 What is an adjustment layer and what are its unique benefits?

▶ **Review answers**

1 Photoshop Elements must be in Full Edit mode to copy a layer. You can select the layer you want to duplicate in the Layers palette, and then choose Layer > Duplicate Layer. Alternatively, drag the layer to the New Layer button in the Layers palette. In either case, you get two identical layers, stacked one above the other.

2 You can adjust the lighting for a photo in either Full Edit, Guided Edit, or Quick Fix mode. In Full Edit, you must use the Enhance > Adjust Lighting menu to open various dialog boxes that contain the controls. Or, you can choose Enhance > Auto Levels, Enhance > Auto Contrast, or Enhance > Adjust Color > Adjust Color Curves. In the Guided Edit mode, choose Lighting and Exposure. In Quick Fix mode, you can use the Lighting palette in the Palette Bin.

3 You cannot rearrange image windows in Quick Fix and Guided Edit modes, which display only one photograph at a time. In Full Edit, there are several ways you can arrange them. One is to choose Window > Images, and select one of the choices listed there. Another method is to use the maximize or tile windows buttons in the upper right corner of each edit window. A third way is to drag the image window title bar to move an image window, and drag a corner to resize it (provided Maximize mode is not currently active).

4 An adjustment layer does not contain an image. Instead, it modifies some quality of all the layers below it in the Layer palette. For example, a Brightness/ Contrast layer can alter the brightness and contrast of any underlying layers. One advantage of using an adjustment layer instead of adjusting an existing layer directly is that adjustment layers are easily reversible. You can click the eye icon for the adjustment layer to remove the effects instantly, and then restore the eye icon to apply the adjustments again. You can change a setting in the adjustment layer to zero to revert to its original condition.

8 | Repairing and Retouching Images

Images aren't always perfect. Maybe you want to clean dust and scratches off a scanned image, retouch spots and small imperfections on a person's skin, or even hide objects you don't want to appear in your photos. Or perhaps you want to restore an antique photograph.

In this lesson, you will do the following:

- Use the Straighten tool.

- Remove red eyes in the Organizer.

- Retouch wrinkles and skin flaws using the Healing Brush tool.

- Eliminate creases with the Clone Stamp tool.

- Use the Selection Brush tool.

- Mask parts of the image.

The work in this lesson should take you about one hour. The lesson includes four independent exercises, so you can do them all at once or in different work sessions. The projects vary only slightly in length and complexity.

Before you begin, make sure that you have correctly copied the Lessons folder from the CD in the back of this book onto your computer's hard disk. See "Copying the Classroom in a Book files" on page 3.

In this lesson, you will use the CIB Catalog you created earlier in the book. If necessary, open this catalog by choosing File > Catalog and selecting the CIB Catalog in the Catalog Manager dialog box.

Getting started

You can start with any of the three exercises in this lesson, because they are independent of each other in both subject matter and skill level. Some preparation is necessary, however, before you begin to open the files for this lesson.

1   Start Photoshop Elements in Full Edit mode by choosing Edit from the Welcome Screen.

2   Make sure the Editor is in Full Edit mode by clicking the Full tab in Edit panel of the Task pane.

3   Open the Palette Bin and Project Bin, if they are not already open, by choosing Window > Palette Bin and Window > Project Bin. You should see a checkmark next to both menu commands.

4   Review the contents of the Palette Bin, making sure that the Layers palette is visible. If necessary, open this palette from the Window menu (Windows > Layers).

Note: For help with Palette Bin contents, see "Using the Palette Bin" in Lesson 1, "A Quick Tour of Photoshop Elements."

Using the Straighten tool

The Straighten tool enables you to manually specify a new straight edge, which Photoshop Elements then uses as a reference to straighten the image.

1 In the Editor, choose File > Open. In the Lesson08 folder open the file 08_01.jpg, a picture of a group of children. As is often the case when taking photos, the picture is not exactly horizontal.

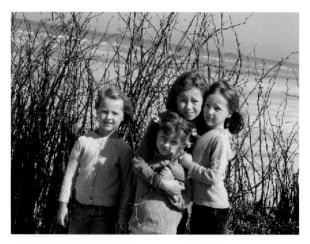

2 In the toolbox, select the Straighten tool ( ).

3 With the Straighten tool, draw a line along the horizon from the top left to the right border. This represents your new straight edge.

4   When you release the pointer, Photoshop Elements straightens the image relative to the edge you've just drawn.

5   In the toolbox, select the Crop tool (⊟). Drag a cropping selection around the image, which is now displayed at an angle, being careful to not draw over the gray area around the image. Then, click the green Commit button in the lower right corner of the selection rectangle.

6   The cropped image features a straight horizon. Choose File > Save As. In the Save As dialog box, navigate to the My CIB Work folder. If selected, deselect the Save in Version Set with Original option. Choose JPEG from the Format menu, name the file **08_01_Straight.jpg**, and then click Save.

7   Click OK in the JPEG options dialog box to accept the default settings.

8   Choose File > Close to close the file.

> 💡 *For some images, you may want to consider using the Image > Rotate > Straighten Image or Image > Rotate > Straighten and Crop Image commands, which perform straightening functions automatically.*

Removing red eye in the Organizer

Red eye is caused by the camera's flash reflection off the subject's retina. You'll see it more often when taking pictures in a darkened room, because the subject's iris is then wide open.

While Photoshop Elements can automatically fix red eyes when you bring photos into the Organizer (see the *Automatically Fixing Red Eyes* sidebar in Lesson 2), here you'll use a command in the Organizer for fixing red eyes. Lesson 6 discusses the tools available in the Editor to fix red eye (see *Using automatic Red Eye Fix in the Editor* and *The Red Eye Removal tool* in Lesson 6).

You can remove red eye from one or more selected photos while viewing them in the Photo Browser.

1   In the Editor, click the Organizer button to load the Organizer workspace. If necessary, click the Show All button above the Photo Browser.

2   In the Keyword Tags palette, click the Find box next to the Lesson 8 keyword tag. Click to select the file 08_02.jpg, a picture of a startled child staring straight into the camera. If necessary, choose View > Show File Names.

3   In the Fix panel of the Task pane, click the Auto Red Eye Fix button. Or, if you prefer to use a menu command, choose Edit > Auto Red Eye Fix. Both commands trigger the same process.

A progress window will appear displaying the progress of the red eye fix.

When the fix is complete, an Auto Fix Red Eye dialog box may appear informing you that a version set was created. Version sets are identified by a version set icon in the upper right corner of an image. *(See illustration on the next page.)*

4   Click OK, to close the Auto Red Eye Fix Complete dialog box.

5   If not already selected, click to select the image in the Photo Browser. To view the results in the Editor, click the Editor button located near the top right corner of the Organizer window, and then choose Full Edit from the menu. Or, click the Full Edit button in the Fix panel of the Task pane.

6   In the Editor, select the Zoom tool (🔍) from the toolbox. Select Zoom In from the tool options bar, and then click to zoom in to view the results of the Auto Fix Red Eye feature. The red is now removed from the child's eyes.

7   Choose File > Close to close the file and return to the Organizer.

Removing wrinkles and spots

Retouching photographs is both a craft and an art. In this exercise, you'll try several ways to smooth out laugh lines and wrinkles, and blend skin tones.

Preparing the file for editing

Before you actually start retouching, you'll set up the layers you need to do the work. By saving the file with a new name, you'll make it easy to identify it later as your work file.

1　Using the Organizer, find and select the file 08_03.jpg, which is tagged with the Lesson 8 keyword tag. Then, click the Editor button located near the upper right corner of the Organizer window and choose Full Edit from the menu that appears.

2　In the Layers palette of the Editor, drag the Background layer to the New Layer button () in the Layers palette to create another layer, which will be called Background copy.

3　Choose File > Save As, and then save the file in Photoshop (PSD) format as **08_03_Work** in the My CIB Work folder. If Save in Version Set with Original is selected, deselect it before you click Save. Make sure the Layers checkbox is selected.

Now you're ready to start improving the photo by creating smoother skin and natural looking skin tones using the Healing Brush tool.

Fixing Blemishes

There are three main tools in Photoshop Elements to fix flaws in your photos:

The Spot Healing brush tool

The Spot Healing Brush is the easiest way to remove wrinkles and small imperfections in your photos. You can either click once on a blemish, or click and drag to smooth it away. By blending the information of the surrounding area into the problem spot, imperfections are made indistinguishable.

The Healing Brush tool

The Healing Brush fixes large areas of imperfections when you drag over them. You need to define the part of your photo to use as source for the material you want to blend in. With this flexibility you can even remove objects from a uniform background, such as a person in a corn field.

The Clone Stamp tool

Instead of blending in the repair, the Clone Stamp tool paints with a sample of an image. You can use the Clone Stamp tool to duplicate objects, remove image imperfections, or paint over objects in your photo. This tool is useful if you wish to completely hide an object, rather than remove it by blending information over the top of it.

Using the Healing Brush tool

While using the Healing Brush tool (✏), make sure the Background copy layer is still active.

1 Zoom in on the upper half of the photo, as you'll be retouching the skin area around the woman's eyes.

2 Select the Healing Brush tool, which is grouped with the Spot Healing Brush tool in the toolbox.

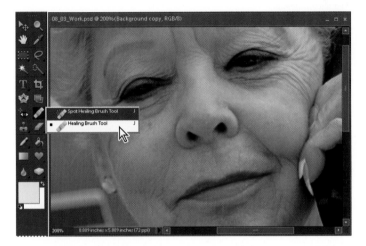

3 In the tool options bar, select the following options:

- For Brush, click the small arrow to open the palette and set the Diameter at 15 px.

- For Mode, select Normal.

- For Source, select Sampled.

- Deselect Aligned and All Layers, if they are selected.

4   Alt+click with the Healing Brush tool on the woman's right cheek to establish that area as the reference texture.

Note: Until you perform this essential step, the Healing Brush tool can't work. If you switch to another tool and then back to the Healing Brush, you must repeat this step.

5   Draw a short horizontal stroke under the left eye. As you drag, it looks as if you're painting dark spots, but when you release the mouse button, the highlight color disappears and skin tones fill in the area.

Note: Be very careful to keep your brush strokes short. Longer strokes may produce unacceptable results. If that happens, choose Edit > Undo Healing Brush, or use the Undo History palette to backtrack. Or, try just clicking instead of dragging. Also, make sure that Aligned is not selected in the tool options bar.

6   Continue to use the Healing Brush to smooth the skin on the face, hands, and neck. Avoid the areas close to the eyes or near the edges of the face. Feel free to reestablish the reference texture by Alt+clicking in other parts of the face to use different skin tones.

7   Use the Undo History palette to quickly undo a series of steps. Every action you perform on the file is recorded in chronological order from top to bottom of the palette. To restore the file to an earlier state, simply select that action in the Undo History palette (Window > Undo History). If you change your mind before making any other

changes, you can select a later step in the Undo History palette and restore the image to that phase of your work.

The Healing Brush tool copies texture, not color. In this case, it samples the colors from the area it brushes and arranges those colors according to the texture of the reference area (the cheek). Consequently, the Healing Brush tool appears to be smoothing the skin. So far, the results are not convincingly realistic, but you'll work on that in the next topic.

💡 *As an alternative to using the Healing Brush, use the Spot Healing Brush to remove spots and small imperfections in your photo. You can either click, or click and drag to smooth away imperfections in an area.*

Refining the healing brush results

In this next exercise, you'll use another texture tool to finish your work on this image.

1   Use the Navigator palette (Window > Navigator) to zoom in to the area of the woman's face around the eyes and mouth.

2 In the toolbox, select the Blur tool (💧). Then, set the brush diameter in the tool options bar to approximately 13 px.

3 Drag the Blur tool over the laugh lines around the eyes and mouth.

4 In the tool options bar, reduce the Blur tool brush diameter to 7 px. Drag across the lips to smooth them out, avoiding the edges.

5 Using the Healing Brush and Blur tools, continue working on the image until you have eliminated most of the lines and blended the skin tones. Use the Navigator palette to change the zoom level and shift the focus as needed.

6 In the Layers palette, change the Opacity of the Background Copy layer to about 70%, using your own judgment to set the exact percentage.

Compare your results to the original, retouched (100% Opacity), and final results illustrated below.

Note: In the Editor, you can toggle the visibility of the retouched Background copy layer to compare the original file with your edited version.

Original

Retouched (100% Opacity)

Retouched (70% Opacity)

Extensive retouching can leave skin looking artificially smooth, like molded plastic. Reducing the opacity of the retouched layer gives the skin a more realistic look by allowing some of the wrinkles on the original Background layer to show through. Although they are slightly visible, they are softened.

7   Choose File > Save to save your changes, and then close the file and return to the Organizer.

In this exercise, you learned how to set an appropriate source for the Healing Brush tool, and then use the texture of that source to repair flaws in another area of the photograph. You also used the Blur tool to smooth textures, and finished with an opacity change to create a more realistic look.

Restoring a damaged photograph

All sorts of nasty things can happen to precious old photographs—or precious new photographs, for that matter. The scanned image of an antique photograph you'll use in this project is challenging, because of a large crease in the original print, and other flaws.

With Photoshop Element tools and features, you have the power to restore this picture to a convincing simulation of its original condition. There's no magic pill that fixes significant damage in one or two keystrokes. However, for important heirloom pictures, the work is worth the effort, and we think you'll be impressed with what you can accomplish in this project.

Preparing a working copy of the image file

Your first job is to set up the file and layers for the work you'll do in this project.

1   Using the Organizer, find and select the file 08_04.psd, the scanned photo of the twin babies, tagged with the Lesson 8 keyword tag. Then, click the Editor button and choose Full Edit from the menu that appears.

2   In the Editor, choose File > Save As. In the Save As dialog box, type **08_04_Work** as the File Name and select Photoshop (PSD) as the Format. For Save In, select the My CIB Work folder. If Save in Version Set with Original is selected, deselect it before you click Save.

3   Choose Layer > Duplicate Layer and in the Duplicate Layer dialog box, click OK to accept the default name.

Using the Clone Stamp tool to fill in missing areas

The first thing you'll do is to eliminate the creases. The Clone Stamp tool paints with a sample of an image, which you can use to remove image imperfections, or paint over certain areas of the image, like the creases.

1   With the help of the Navigator palette or the Zoom tool, zoom in on the crease in the lower right corner.

2   In the toolbox, select the Clone Stamp tool ( ), which is grouped with the Pattern Stamp tool.

3   On the left end of the tool options bar, click the triangle and choose Reset Tool from the menu that appears.

Reset Tool reinstates the default values—Size: 21 px, Mode: Normal, Opacity: 100%, and the Aligned option is selected.

4   In the tool options bar, select from the Basic Brushes a hard, mechanical brush with the size of 48 pixels. As Mode choose Normal and set Opacity to 100%. Select Aligned.

5   Move the Clone Stamp tool to the left of the crease at the bottom of the picture. Hold down the Alt key and click to set the source position. Centering the source on a horizontal line makes it easier to line up the brush for cloning. The tool duplicates the pixels at this sample point in your image as you paint.

Note: If necessary, you can reset the source by Alt+clicking again in a different location as well as click the Undo button (**).

6   Move the brush over the damaged area so that it is centered at the same horizontal position as the source reference point. Click and drag sidewards over the crease to copy the source image onto the damaged area. As you drag, crosshairs appear, indicating where the source is—that is, the area that the Clone Stamp tool is copying. To repair the upper part of the crease, set the source position in the area above the crease and drag downwards.

7   Continue to drag the brush over the crease-damaged area, resetting the source position if necessary, until the repair is complete.

The crosshairs follow the movement of the brush. Because you selected the Aligned option in the tool options bar, the crosshairs maintain the same distance and angle to the brush that you set when you made the first brush stroke.

8   Now, smooth out the crease in the upper right side corner. For this exercise the Healing Brush tool () is the better option, because the crease is quite prominent, causing significant variations in the background color. The Healing brush with a small brush size is also the right tool to restore the defect caused by a large white speck on the ear of the baby to your right.

9   Choose File > Save to save your changes.

Using the Selection Brush tool

Next step with this project is to use the Dust & Scratches filter to remove the stray dots and frayed edges of the scanned image. This filter smoothes out the pixels in a way that puts the image just slightly out of focus. That's OK for the background, but the subject matter—the children—should be kept as detailed and as sharp as possible. To do that, you'll need to create a selection that includes only the areas you want to blur.

1 In the toolbox, select the Selection Brush tool (✐), which is grouped with the Quick Selection tool. Be careful to not select a painting brush tool by mistake.

2 In the tool options bar, select a round brush shape and set the size to about 60 pixels. You may need to increase the brush size after the previous exercise.

Leave the other options at the default values: Mode should be set to Selection and Hardness should be set to 100%.

3 Drag the brush along the frayed edges of the photograph to select those areas. Then, increase or decrease the brush size as needed and continue painting the selection to include all the frayed edges and most of the background behind the children.

Note: Don't try to be too precise; it's OK if some of your strokes go over onto the children because you'll fix that in the next topic.

4   Choose Select > Save Selection.

5   Name the new selection **Backdrop** and click OK to close the Save Selection dialog box.

The Selection Brush tool is an intuitive way to create a complex selection. In images like this one, where there are no unique color blocks, few sharp boundaries between pictured items, and few crisp geometric shapes, the Selection Brush tool is especially useful.

Just as the Spot Healing Brush provides a quicker alternative to the Healing Brush tool, the Quick Selection Brush tool (✎) is a faster alternative to using the Selection Brush tool. The Quick Selection Brush tool automatically makes selection based on color and texture when you click or click-drag an area.

Another advantage of the Selection Brush tool is that it is very forgiving. For example, you can hold down the Alt while dragging to remove areas from a selection. Or, you can use the tool in Mask mode, which is another intuitive way of adding to the areas outside the selection, as you'll try next.

What is a mask?

A mask is the opposite of a selection. A selection is an area that you can alter; everything outside the selection is unaffected by editing changes. A mask is an area that's protected from changes, just like the solid areas of a stencil or the masking tape you'd put on window glass at home before you paint the wooden trim.

Another difference between a mask and a selection is the way Photoshop Elements presents them visually. You're familiar with the flashing line of black and white dashes that signal a selection marquee. A mask appears as a colored, semi-transparent overlay on the image. You can change the color of the mask overlay using the Overlay Color option that appears in the tool options bar when the Selection Brush tool is set to operate in Mask mode.

Refining a saved selection

As you progress through this book, you're gathering lots of experience with saving selections. In this procedure, you'll amend a saved selection and replace it with your improved version.

1   In the work area, make sure that:

•   The Backdrop selection is still active in the image window. If it is not active, choose Selection > Load Selection, and choose the saved selection by name, before clicking OK.

•   The Selection Brush tool (🖌) is still selected in the toolbox.

2   In the tool options bar, select Mask in the Mode menu.

You now see a semi-transparent, colored overlay in the unselected areas of the image. This represents the image mask, which covers the protected areas.

3   Examine the image, looking for unmasked areas with details that should be protected, such as places where the Selection Brush strokes extended over onto the children.

Use the Navigator palette slider or Zoom tool (🔍) to adjust your view of the image, if necessary.

4   Reduce the brush size of the Selection Brush to about 30 pixels, and then use the brush to paint any areas you want to mask. Press the Alt key while painting to remove an area from the mask.

In this mode, the Selection Brush tool creates the mask rather than the selection.

5 Switch back and forth between Selection and Mask modes, making corrections until you are satisfied with the selection—or mask for that matter.

Your goal is to mask areas that contain fine details you want to preserve.

6 Choose Select > Save Selection. In the Save Selection dialog box, choose Backdrop from the Selection menu. Then, under Operation, select Replace Selection and click OK.

7 With the Selection Brush tool still active, make sure that in the tool options bar you have Selection—not Mask—selected in the Mode menu. Keep the selection active for the next procedure.

Filtering flaws out of the backdrop area

Now that you've made your selection, you're ready to apply the filter that will soften the selected areas, reducing the tiny scratches and dust specks.

1 If the Backdrop selection is no longer active, choose Select > Load Selection and choose Backdrop before you click OK to close the dialog box.

2 Choose Filter > Noise > Dust & Scratches.

3 In the Dust & Scratches dialog box, make sure that Preview is selected, and then drag the Radius slider to 8 pixels and the Threshold slider to 10 levels. Move the dialog box so that you can see most of the image window, but do not close it yet.

4 Examine the results in the image window. The frayed edges of the image should be repaired and the stray dust and tiny scratches eliminated. Move the cursor inside the thumbnail and drag with the hand icon to change the preview area that is displayed.

5 Make adjustments to the Radius and Threshold values until you are satisfied with the results, and then click OK to close the Dust & Scratches dialog box.

6 Choose Select > Deselect, and then choose File > Save to save your work.

The Dust & Scratches filter does a good job of clearing away spots created by flaws on the negative. However, it doesn't repair damage to the areas outside the selection.

Finishing up the project

While you could spend longer working on this picture, the quality is now acceptable for most purposes. You'll fix just a few more areas before leaving this project.

1 Double-click the Hand tool (🖐) to zoom out so that you can see the entire image. Alternatively, you can use the Navigator palette or the Zoom tool.

2 Examine the entire image, looking for dark or light flecks created by dust on the negative, especially on the dark areas of the photograph.

3 In the toolbox, select the Blur tool (💧) and type **40 px** for Size in the tool options bar.

4 Click or drag the tool over any dust spots to blend them into the surrounding area.

5 Review all areas of the image. If you see flaws that you want to fix, make any additional repairs or corrections.

Original   *Retouched*

6 Choose File > Save, and then close the file.

Congratulations, you have finished this project. In this exercise, you've used blurring and a filter to hide spots, flecks, and texture flaws. You've also cloned one area of an image to repair an area that's been damaged. You've used the Selection Brush tool to create selections in two modes: Selection and Mask. Along the way, you've seen how to reset a tool to its default settings.

Review

▶ Review questions

1   What tools can you use to fix the red eye phenomenon created by some flash cameras?

2   How can you quickly undo a series of edit steps?

3   What are the similarities and differences between using the Healing Brush and the Spot Healing Brush tools to retouch photos?

4   Why is it necessary to make a selection (e.g., using the Magic Selection tool) before applying the Dust & Scratches filter to restore a damaged photograph?

5   What is the difference between a selection and a mask?

▶ Review answers

1   You can choose to automatically fix red eye when importing photos into the catalog. Simply select Automatically Fix Red Eye where available in the various import dialog boxes. To fix red eye after the photos have been imported, choose Edit > Auto Red Eye Fix in the Organizer. In either the Full Edit or Quick Fix mode of the Editor, choose Enhance > Auto Red Eye Fix. Finally, the Red Eye Removal tool located in the toolbox enables you to adjust some parameters while fixing red eye.

2   Use the Undo History palette to quickly undo a series of steps. Every action you perform on the file is recorded in chronological order from top to bottom of the palette. To restore the file to an earlier state, simply select that action in the Undo History palette. If you change your mind before making any other changes, you can select a later step in the Undo History palette and restore the image to that phase of your work.

3   Both tools copy from one part of an image to another. The Spot Healing Brush tool, especially with the Proximity Match option selected, enables you to remove blemishes more quickly than does the Healing Brush, because it only involves clicking and/or dragging on an imperfection to smooth it. The Healing

Brush is more customizable, but requires Alt+clicking to establish a reference texture.

4 Because the Dust & Scratches filter smoothes out pixels in an image by putting them slightly out of focus, you should create a selection that includes only the areas you need to blur. Otherwise, your subject matter won't be as detailed and sharp as possible.

5 A mask is the opposite of a selection. The selection is the area that you can alter; everything outside the selection is unaffected by editing changes. A mask is the area that's protected from changes.

Another difference between a mask and a selection is the way Photoshop Elements presents them visually. You're familiar with the flashing line of black and white dashes that signal a selection marquee. A mask appears as a colored, semi-transparent overlay on the image. You can change the color of the mask overlay using the Overlay Color option that appears in the tool options bar when the Selection Brush tool is set to operate in Mask mode.

9 | Working with Text

Adding a message to your photos is yet another way to make your images and compositions more memorable and personal. Photoshop Elements provides you with tools to add crisp, flexible, and editable type to your pictures. Whether you need straightforward, classic typography or wild effects and wacky colors, it's all possible. In this lesson, you'll learn how to do the following:

- Add a border to an image by changing the canvas size.

- Format, add, and edit text.

- Manipulate text using Layer Styles.

- Warp text.

- Tile images.

- Move image layers independently.

- Hide, reveal, and delete layers.

- Transfer a layer from one image to another.

- Merge two layers into a single layer.

- Apply a type clipping mask.

Before you begin, make sure that you have correctly copied the Lessons folder from the CD in the back of this book onto your computer's hard disk. See "Copying the Classroom in a Book files" on page 3.

In this lesson, you will use the CIB Catalog you created earlier in the book. If necessary, open this catalog by choosing File > Catalog and selecting the CIB Catalog in the Catalog Manager dialog box.

Getting started

This lesson includes several projects. Each project builds on the skills learned in the previous projects. Most people need about one to two hours to complete this lesson.

This lesson assumes that you are already familiar with general features of the Photoshop Elements work area, and that you recognize the two ways in which you can use Photoshop Elements: the Editor and the Organizer. If you discover that you need more background information as you proceed, see Photoshop Elements Help, or the Tutorials available on the Welcome Screen.

Placing a text label on an image

This project involves typing, formatting, and arranging text on a photograph. The goal is to add a greeting and create a border for the photo so it can be printed and mounted in a picture frame.

The original file (left) and completed project file (right).

About Type

A font is a collection characters—letters, numerals, punctuation marks, and symbols—in a particular typeface, which share design characteristics such as size, weight, and style. A typeface family is a collection of similar fonts designed to be used together. One example is the Myriad typeface family, which is a collection of fonts in a number of styles including Regular, Bold, Italic, Condensed and other variations. Other typeface families might consist of different font style variations.

Font family	
Myriad Pro	Times New Roman
Font style	
Regular, **Bold**, *Italic*, Condensed	Regular, **Bold**, *Italic*

Traditionally, font sizes are measured in points, but can also be specified in millimeters or inches, as with large lettering on signs, for example. The most common formats for computer fonts are Type 1 PostScript, TrueType, and OpenType.

Each font conveys a feeling or mood. Some are playful or amusing, some are serious and businesslike, while others might convey an impression of elegance and sophistication. To get a feel for which typeface best suits your project, it's good to try out several fonts. One way to find out more about type is to go to www.adobe.com/type. Adobe Type offers more than 2,200 fonts from the world's leading type designers, which you can browse by categories such as style, use, theme, classification, and designers. This will make it easy to find the perfect font for any assignment. You can even type in your sample copy and compare different fonts.

Using the Organizer to find and open tagged files

To make it easier to find the files you are now going to work with, we've tagged them with the name of the appropriate lesson.

1   Open Adobe Photoshop Elements, and choose Edit in the Welcome screen.

2   Choose File > Open, and open the file 09_01.jpg in your Lessons09 folder, a picture of a family at the beach.

3   Make sure you are working in Full Edit mode.

Adding an uneven border

In this procedure you'll enlarge the canvas—the area on which the image appears—without increasing the size of the image. The canvas size is usually the same as the image size for digital photographs, but by enlarging it you can add a border. The border area takes on the Background color, which is comparable to the paper underlying a photographic print.

You'll create this border in two phases and give it precise dimensions.

1   Choose Image > Resize > Canvas Size.

2   In the Canvas Size dialog box, complete the following steps:

•   Select the Relative check box.

•   For Width, type **0.5** and select inches from the menu.

- For Height type **0.5**, and select inches from the menu.

- Leave the default setting for the center square in the Anchor diagram, and White from the current Background color as the Canvas extension color.

- Click OK to close the dialog box and apply the changes. A white border now surrounds the image.

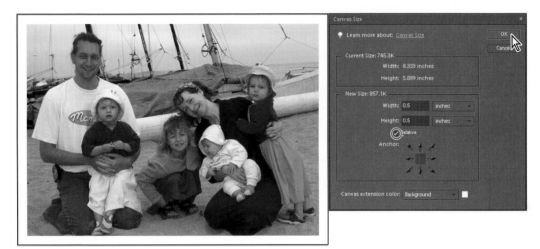

3   Now let's extend the border below the image where the greeting should go. Choose Image > Resize > Canvas Size again. Confirm that the Relative check box remains selected, and then enter the following options:

- In the Anchor diagram, select the center square in the top row.

- Confirm Width is set to 0, or enter **0** now.

- For Height, type **1**.

- Leave all other settings unchanged and click OK.

(See illustration on the next page.)

Now the border around the image has become wider at the bottom, providing a perfect stage for the text you'll add next.

Adding a text layer

With the Horizontal Type and Vertical Type tools you can place type anywhere on your image. The text you type is automatically entered on a new type layer. You can later resize the text if necessary without losing quality since the font outlines are stored as vector images.

Distinguishing between Pixels and Vectors

Computer graphics can be divided into two types: pixel-based images (bit mapped, or raster images, primarily created by cameras and scanners), and vector images (constructed with drawing programs).

Pixel-based images, like photos, are made up of pixels, or little squares (you can detect them when you zoom in). Adobe Photoshop is a widely used program that lets you manipulate pixels. To produce a medium quality print of your pictures for print, make sure that the file is at least 250 ppi (pixels per inch), while for viewing on screen, 72 ppi is fine

Vector images consist of artwork formed from paths, like a technical line drawing, the outline of a logo, or type. One big advantage of vector images is that they can be enlarged or reduced without losing detail.

In the tool options bar, which will appear once the Type tool is your active tool, you will choose formatting for the type. This includes the font family, font size, text color, paragraph style, and other text attributes.

1   In the toolbox, select the Horizontal Type tool (T).

2   In the tool options bar, select the following from the menus:

•   For font family, select MyriadPro.

•   For font style, select Bold.

•   For font size, type **44** pt.

•   Leave the default setting for the Leading (the space between two lines of text) at Auto.

•   To set the text color, click the triangle beside the Color option to open the color menu palette. Then, select Pure Cyan Blue as Color.

•   For paragraph alignment, select Center Text (≡).

3 Click in the frame area below the picture to set the cursor and type in all uppercase **GREETINGS FROM SANTA CRUZ.**

Note: Do not press the Enter or Return keys on the central part of your keyboard to accept text changes. When the Type tool is active, these keys add a line break in the text. To create a new line of text, press Enter.

4   Click the Commit button (✔) in the tool options bar to accept the text. Or, press Enter on the numeric keypad. Don't worry about the exact position of the text in the image or any typing errors, because you'll correct those later in this project.

(See illustration on next page.)

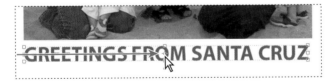

Notice in the Layers palette in the Palette Bin on the right of your work area, that the image is now made up of two layers: a Background, which contains the image and is locked, and the text layer, which contains the message you just typed. Most of the text layer is transparent, so only the text itself blocks your view of the Background layer.

5 Next is to center the type below the image. Select the Move tool (⊕) in the toolbox.

6 Place the cursor inside the text so that the cursor turns into a solid black arrowhead (▶) and drag the text so that it is visually centered along the lower border of the image.

Note: Adobe Photoshop Elements 6.0 also includes other tools for adding text to your images. Throughout the remainder of this lesson, the term Type tool always refers to the Horizontal Type tool, which is the default type tool.

Adding a quick border

When precision isn't important for the canvas-size enlargement, you can use the Crop tool to quickly add a border to an image.

1 Select the Zoom tool (🔍) and zoom out by holding down the Alt key and clicking. The cursor will change from a magnifying glass with a plus sign (🔍) to one with a minus sign (🔍). If necessary, click again until you can see some of the gray pasteboard surrounding the image.

2 Select the Crop tool (🔲) and drag a rectangle within the image—size doesn't matter at this point.

3 Drag the corner handles of the crop marquee outside the image area onto the pasteboard to define the size and shape of border that you want to create.

4 After you have defined the new size for the image and border, click the Commit button (✔) on the tool options bar to apply the change. Or, click the Cancel button (⊘) next to the Commit button if you don't want to crop the image. The Background Color fills in the newly expanded canvas.

Editing in a text layer

Adding vector-based text is a nondestructive process, so your original image is not overwritten by the text. If you save your file in the native Photoshop (PSD) format, you can reopen it and move, edit, or delete the text layer without affecting the image.

Using the Type tool is much like typing in a word processing application. If you want to change attributes such as font style or text color, select the characters you want to change, and then adjust the settings.

1   If necessary, choose View > Zoom In to enlarge the image until you can comfortably read the text you added in the previous exercise.

2   Confirm that the text layer GREETINGS FROM SANTA CRUZ is still selected in the Layers palette and the Type tool (T) is active.

3   Click to the right of "CRUZ" and press Enter to add a line break in the text. Then type (this time in upper and lowercase) **The Evans Family,** so that the text reads:
"GREETINGS FROM SANTA CRUZ
The Evans Family".

Now we want to change the font style, reduce the font size and change the color of the second line of text.

4   Move the cursor to the beginning of the second line of text. Click and drag over the text to select all the text in the second line.

5   In the tool options bar, select MyriadPro Regular and choose 30 pt as font size.

6   Click the arrow beside the Color option and select a black color swatch. When choosing your own colors, be certain to select colors that are easy to read against the background color. Press the Return key to close the Swatches palette.

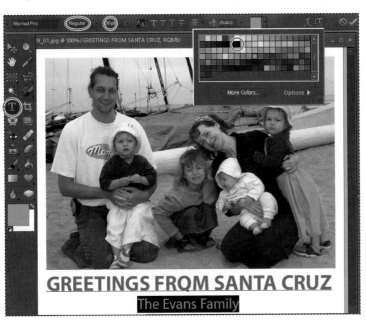

Note: By clicking the Color sample instead of the arrow next to it in the tool options bar, you can open the Color Picker, which is a different way to select colors.

7 If necessary, using the Type tool, correct any typing errors you may have made. To do this:

- Click once to move the insertion point to another position within the text, or use the arrow keys to move the cursor forward or back.

- Click and drag to select multiple characters.

- Type to add text or to overwrite selected characters.

- Press Backspace or Delete to erase characters.

8 Click the Commit button (✔) in the tool options bar to accept your editing changes.

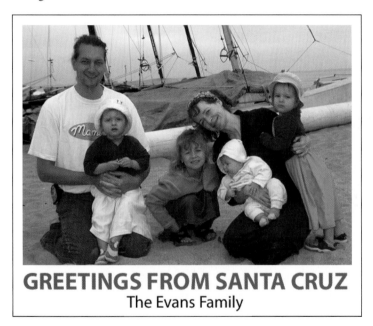

Saving your work file

In this procedure, you'll save your work file so you can review it later.

1 Choose File > Save. The Save As dialog box opens.

2 Navigate to and open the My CIB Work folder.

3 In the Save As dialog box, enter the following settings:

• As File name, type **09_01_Work**.

• As Format, confirm that Photoshop (PSD) is selected.

4 Under Save Options, confirm that the Include in the Organizer option is selected, and—if selected—deselect Save in Version Set with Original.

5 Review your settings and click the Save button. If the Photoshop Elements Format Options dialog box appears, keep Maximize Compatibility selected and click OK.

6 Choose File > Close.

Bravo, you've finished your first text project. In this section, you've formatted and edited text, and seen how layers work independently in an image. You've also enlarged the canvas size without stretching the image itself.

Overlaying text on an image

In the first project of this lesson, you've preserved the layering of the work files by saving in a file format that supports layers. This provides you with the flexibility to make changes to the images after they have been saved, without having to rebuild the image from the beginning, or modify the original image. The layers have kept the text and shapes separate from the original image.

In this project, you'll do what professional photographic studios sometimes do to protect proprietary images—stamp a copyright notice over the photo. You will apply a style to a text layer so that it looks as if the word is set on clear glass overlaid on a print of the images.

Creating a new document for the text

You'll start by preparing the text in its own file. In this procedure, you'll see a gray-and-white checkerboard pattern. This pattern indicates 100% transparency, where an area or complete layer acts like a pane of clear glass on which you can add text or graphics.

1   Make sure you're still in Full Edit mode. In the Editor, choose File > New > Blank File.

2   In the New dialog box, enter the following settings:

- For Name, type **Overlay**.

- For Width, type **600**, and select pixels.

- For Height, type **600**, and select pixels.

- For Resolution, type **72**, and select pixels/inch.

- For Color Mode, select RGB Color.

- For Background Contents, select Transparent.

- Review your settings to make sure they are correct and click OK.

The image window shows only a checkerboard pattern. If it does not, choose Edit > Undo and repeat Step 2, being careful to select Transparent from the Background Contents menu. The pattern represents the transparent background that you selected when creating the file.

3   Select the Type tool (T), and then in the tool options bar, set the following text attributes:

- Arial as font family (a sans serif font is best for the purpose of this project)

- Bold as font style

- 120 pt as font size

- Left aligned as text alignment

- Black as text color

4   Click near the left side of the image window and type **copyright 2007**. Click the green Commit button (✔) in the tool options bar to accept the text you've typed.

5   Select the Move tool (▸⊕). Click and drag the text to center it in the image window.

6   Position the Move tool outside a corner of the text bounding box so that the cursor changes to a curved, double-ended arrow (⤿), and then click and drag counter-clockwise around the center to rotate the text so it appears at a slight angle.

Note: You can also resize or reshape the text by dragging corners of the bounding box. Because Photoshop Elements text layers are vector shapes, based on mathematics rather than pixels the letter shapes remain smooth even if you drag the corners of the bounding box to enlarge the text. If you tried this with bitmap text, you'd see jagged, stair-step edges in the enlarged text.

7   Click the Commit button (✔) near the lower left corner of the selection rectangle.

Applying a Layer Style to the text layer

Next, you'll work with a Layer Style. Layer Styles are combinations of adjustments that you apply in one easy action to your text layer. Photoshop Elements gives you a wide variety of choices,

1   In the Palette Bin, locate the Effects palette. If the palette is not displayed in your work area, choose Window > Effects. If necessary, click the triangle in the upper left corner of the Effects palette to expand it.

2   At the top of the Effects palette, select Layer style (■), and then use the scroll bar to select the second last effect, Wow Plastic.

3 If necessary, scroll down to see the end of the list of available choices, and then double-click the Wow Plastic White effect thumbnail to apply it to the selected text layer. As an alternative, you can drag the effect over your text layer image.

Layer Styles keep text editable. Therefore, in the Layers palette, the Copyright text layer thumbnail still displays the T icon (T) for text. Later on, if you wish to change the year of the copyright, for example, you can simply type again in the text layer—with the same Layer style already applied. Notice the Layer style icon (*fx*), which tells you that a layer style has been applied. Generally it's a good idea to make all text editing changes before applying styles or effects to text layers.

4 Choose File > Save to the My CIB Work folder. If the Photoshop Elements Format Options dialog box appears, keep Maximize Compatibility selected, and then click OK.

Adding the text to multiple images

Now that you've prepared the text, you'll place it onto different images you might want to mark with the copy protection message.

1   Click the Organizer (⊞) on the shortcuts bar to switch to the Organizer.

2   On the Tags palette, click the Find boxes for Lesson 9 to help you find the images you'll use for this project.

3   Control-click to select the four images of paintings called 09_02.jpg, 09_03.jpg, 09_04.jpg, and 09_05.jpg. Then, click the Editor button (✏) and choose Full Edit.

4   To view and arrange multiple windows, choose Window > Images > Tile.

💡 *To view the same section (e.g. upper left corner, center, lower right corner) of all open photos, choose Window > Images > Match Location. The view in all windows shifts to match the active (frontmost) image. The zoom level does not change.*

5   To fully view the images, select the overlay.psd and change the view from 66% (or whatever your default setting) to 30% by typing **30** into the left corner of the image.

6   With the image still active, select Window > Images > Match Zoom.

7   In the Photo Bin (the row of thumbnails across the bottom of the work area), select the Overlay.psd to make it the active file.

8   To make the overlay more transparent, reduce the opacity to 50% either by typing **50** into the box, or by dragging the upcoming slider to the left.

9   Hold down the Shift key, and then drag from the Layers palette the layer thumbnail for the Copyright 2007 text layer and drop it onto the first picture, called 09_02.jpg.

10   You can now see the image of the painting with the copyright notice as a semitransparent overlay. Repeat the previous step, dragging the text onto the two remaining images, 09_03.jpg, 09_04.jpg and 09_05.jpg. Note that you can position the bounding box with the text on each image individually.

11   In the Editor window, click to select the Overlay.psd document containing only the text. Choose File > Close. When asked to Save, click Yes, and then enter the name **Overlay**, and save the file as a Photoshop (PSD) format in the My CIB Work folder on your hard disk. If the Photoshop Elements Format Options dialog box appears, keep Maximize Compatibility selected and click OK.

12   Choose File > Close All.

Done! In this project, you've created a new Photoshop (PSD) format document without an image and added text to that document. You've copied a layer from that document to other image files by dragging it from the Layers palette to the image windows. You've used the Effects palette to apply a Layer Style to the text layer.

Using Layer Styles and distortions

In this next exercise you'll have more fun with text using type distortions and other effects. For this you will apply exciting changes, still preserving the Type layer as text.

Adding the subject text and a layer style

Your first task is to find and open the image file for this project and add the text.

1   Click the Organizer button (▦) located near the top right corner of the Editor window to switch to the Organizer.

2   In the Keyword Tags palette, click the Find box next to the Lesson 9 keyword tag, and then click to select the file 09_06.jpg, a view of a cloudy sky.

3   Click the Editor button, and then choose Full Edit from the menu that appears.

4   In the toolbox, select the Type tool (T) and make the following selections in the tool options bar to set the text attributes:

• For the font family and style, select a bold sans serif font like Impact (as alternatives, choose Arial Bold or Arial Black).

- For the font size, type **120 pt** and press Enter to accept this setting.
- For text alignment, select Center text (≡).
- In the color palette, Set the text color to Pastel Cyan Blue.

5 Using the Type tool, click near the center of the image. In all lower upper case, type **MAYBE**.

6 Click the Commit button (✔) in the tool options bar to accept the text.

7 Choose the Move tool (▶⊕). Click and drag the text to center it as shown in the illustration below.

8 Open the Effects palette by clicking the little triangle next to Effects, select Layer style (■), and stay in the first category named Bevels.

9 Select the last effect in the second row, called Simple Sharp Outer.

10 In the Layers palette, change the opacity to 75% by either typing **75**, or by dragging the slider that appears when you click the triangle next to the value.

11 Save your file into your My CIB Work folder and name it 09_06_Work. Make sure the Layers box is selected.

Warping text

Stretching and skewing text into unusual shapes is incredibly easy in Photoshop Elements. In fact, it is so easy to apply those effects that one needs to be careful not to overuse them.

1 With the Type tool still selected, click anywhere on the text "MAYBE" in the image window.

Note: Highlighting any part of the text isn't necessary, because warping applies to the entire text layer.

2 In the tool options bar, click the Create warped text button () to open the Warp Text dialog box.

3 From the Style menu, select the Fisheye effect.

4 Confirm that Horizontal is chosen for the orientation of the effect and set the Bend value to **+80%**. Then, click OK to close the Warp Text dialog box.

5 The text of MAYBE is still editable. You can check this out by dragging the Type tool over the word to select it, and then typing over it—just make sure the Type tool is still selected.

6   If you changed the text in the previous step, change it back to MAYBE by typing over it.

7   Choose File > Save.

Creating an unstylized copy of the text layer

For the next part of the lesson, you will experiment with an effect that needs your type layer to be simplified, meaning you cannot edit the text anymore. For this you will create two versions of the finished artwork on separate layers.

1   In the Layers palette, select the text layer. Then, click the More menu in the upper right corner of the palette. The palette menu is displayed. From the palette menu, choose Duplicate Layer. Click OK to accept the default layer name MAYBE copy.

💡 You can also drag an existing layer to the New Layer icon (▨) in the Layers palette to create a duplicate layer.

2   Click the eye icon (👁) to the left of the MAYBE layer. The layer becomes invisible in the image window.

3   In the Layers palette, change the opacity of the MAYBE copy layer to 100%.

4   Choose Layer > Layer Style > Clear Layer Style.

The warped text now appears again in solid white, as it did before you applied the Layer Style.

Simplifying and applying a pattern to text

You're now ready to add a different look to the copy of the text layer. Make sure that the MAYBE copy layer is selected in the Layers palette before you begin. One of the interesting things you'll do in this procedure is to lock the transparent pixels on a text layer. This enables you to do all sorts of painting on the shapes in the layer, without having to be careful about the edges.

1   In the toolbox, choose the Clone Stamp tool. In the tool options bar, choose the Pattern Stamp tool icon (🖌).

Note: You can also choose the Pattern Stamp tool by pressing and holding the Clone Stamp tool in the toolbox, and then selecting the Pattern Stamp Tool from the menu that appears.

2   In the tool options bar, select the following:

•   For Size, enter **50** px. The Size setting determines the diameter of the Pattern Stamp tool brush, and can be set by typing in a size, or by clicking the arrow to the right of the value and dragging the slider to change the size.

•   For Mode, confirm that Normal is selected.

•   For Opacity, confirm that 100% is selected.

•   Click on the triangle next to the Pattern box to open the Pattern menu. Then, choose Pink Fur as the pattern.

3 Click with the Pattern Stamp brush on the text. When a message appears, asking if you want to simplify the layer, click OK. After clicking OK, do not click on the text again.

4 In the Layers palette, click the Lock Transparent Pixels button to prevent changes to the transparent areas of the simplified MAYBE copy layer.

Notice that there is now a lock icon on the upper layer, reminding you that you've applied a lock.

5 Paint with the Pattern Stamp tool over the text, applying the pattern as solidly or unevenly as you like.

The pattern affects only the selected layer (the simplified text) and doesn't change any unselected layer, such as the underlying photograph. Because the transparent pixels on the upper MAYBE copy layer are locked they are also protected, so only the simplified text shapes take on the pattern.

After simplifying the text layer, as you've done here, the text can't be edited any more using the Type tool. However, you could still add the appearance of depth or other effects to the patterned text by applying a Layer Style, such as a Bevel or Inner Glow, using the Effects palette.

Hiding and revealing layers

Having placed the two design alternatives of the styled text on different layers, you can use the eye icons in the Layers palette to alternately show one of the two different designs.

1   In the Layers palette, make sure that the eye icons appear in both the Layers palette for the Background layer, and the top layer that you just painted over with the Pattern Stamp tool.

2   Click the eye icon for the top layer, MAYBE copy. This hides the layer and the eye icon is no longer displayed.

3   Click the empty box to the left of the middle MAYBE layer. This causes the eye icon to appear in the Layers palette and also displays the text layer with the warped, blue text in the document window.

The process of switching between layers enables you to quickly decide between different design solutions for a project. Once you've made up your mind, you can simply get rid of the layers you don't want.

Deleting layers and layer styles

In the next steps, you will keep just the original MAYBE text layer and remove the one with the pink fur pattern. Deleting layers that you no longer need reduces the size of your image file.

1   Delete the MAYBE copy layer by clicking the double triangles to open the Layers menu, and then selecting Delete Layer.

(See illustration on the next page.)

💡 *As an alternative, select Delete Hidden Layers from the Layers menu. This way you are able to remove several layers at once.*

2 In the toolbox select the Type tool (T), and then click the Create warped text button (𝕝) to open the Warp Text dialog box.

3 In the Style menu, select None, and then click OK to close the Warp Text dialog box.

4 Now you're back to where you began before using the text warping effect. Choose File > Save and save the file as 09_Work in the My CIB Work folder. Choose Photoshop

(*.PSD, *.PDD) as file format. If Save in Version Set with Original is selected, be sure to deselect it before you click Save. If the Photoshop Elements Format Options dialog box appears, keep Maximize Compatibility selected and click OK.

5   Close your work by selecting File > Close.

In this section, you've applied a Layer Style to text and warped it, which leaves it fully editable but gives it some color and flair. Furthermore you've experimented with filling type with patterns by locking transparent pixels on a layer. Finally, you've kept two potential versions of the final art in one work file.

Working with Paragraph type

With point type, each line of type is independent—the line expands or shrinks as you edit it, but it doesn't wrap to the next line. Point type (the name derives from the fact that it is preceded by a single anchor point) is perfect for small blocks of text like headlines, logos, and headings for Web pages. Probably most of your type entries will use this mode. If you work with larger amounts of text and you want this to wrap automatically, it's best to use the paragraph type mode. By clicking and dragging the type tool you'll create a text bounding box on your image. The bounding box can be easily resized to fit your text perfectly.

Creating type masks

You can have fun with text selection borders by cutting text out of an image to show the background, or pasting the selected text into a new image. All this is possible with the Horizontal or Vertical Type Mask tool.

1   Switch to the Organizer.

2   In the Keyword Tags palette, click the Find box next to the Lesson 9 keyword tag, and then click to select the file 09_07.jpg, an image of two zebras.

3   Click the Editor button, and then choose Full Edit from the menu that appears.

Working with the Type Mask tool

The Type Mask tool (⊤) enables you to fill letter shapes with parts of an image. This can create a much more interesting effect than using plain text with a solid color.

1 In the tool box, select the Horizontal Type Mask tool (𝕋).

2 In the tool options bar, set the following text attributes:
- Stencil as font family (or any sans serif font like Impact or Arial bold is good)
- Bold as font style
- 100 pt as font size

Leave left aligned selected as text alignment. Don't worry about the color attributes as the mask will contain the colors and details of the image.

3 Click near the top of the left zebra's belly and type **ZOO**.

4 The background pattern of zebra stripes shows through the shapes of the letters you just typed, while the rest of the picture is hidden. Select Edit > Copy, and then Edit > Paste. In the Layers palette, notice that the type has been placed onto a new layer. *(See illustration on the next page.)*

5   Hide the background layer by clicking the eye icon (👁).

Although the text cannot be edited anymore, you can still apply a layer style or effect to make it more prominent.

6   Make the Layers 1 your active layer by selecting it, and then open the Effects palette.

7   At the top of the Effects palette, select Layer style (■), and then select Drop Shadows from the menu to the right.

8   In the Drop Shadows palette, select the shadow called Noisy, the second shadow in the second row of effects.

9   Since you don't need the background layer with the zebras, delete it by clicking
Flatten Image in the Layers menu. Click OK in the upcoming dialog box asking whether
to discard the hidden layers.

10   Choose File > Save As and in the Save As dialog box, name the file
09_07_Work. Choose PSD as file format. Navigate to the My CIB Work folder.

Wonderful! You can add this project to your list of accomplishments for the day. In this
part you've learned how to mask type and use it

Review

Review questions

1 What is the advantage of having text on a separate layer?

2 How do you hide a layer without removing it?

3 In the Layers palette, what do the lock icons do and how do they work?

4 What's the difference between point type and paragraph type?

Review answers

1 Because the text remains separate from the image, Photoshop Elements text layers can be edited in later work sessions, just like editable text in other documents.

2 You can hide a layer by clicking the eye icon (👁) next to that layer on the Layers palette. To make the layer visible again, click the empty box where the eye icon should be to restore it.

3 Lock icons prevent changes to a layer. You can click Lock All (🔒) to lock all the pixels on the selected layer, or you can click Lock Transparent Pixels to protect specific areas. To remove a lock, select the locked layer and click the active lock icon to toggle it off. (This does not work for the Background layer, which can be unlocked only by renaming and converting it into an ordinary layer.)

4 Point type is ideal for headlines, logos and other small blocks of text where each line is independent and does not wrap to the next line. Paragraph text is used where you want larger amounts of text to wrap automatically to the next line. The size of the paragraph text bounding box can be easily changed to fit your text perfectly to the job in hand.

10 | Combining Multiple Images

If you're ready to go beyond fixing individual pictures in conventional ways, this lesson is for you. In it you'll venture into the world of multiple images to add an effect, or move a person or object from one photo into another. In this lesson, you will do the following:

• Merge photos into a panorama.

• Use the Photomerge Group Shot tool to create the perfect group shot.

• Crop images.

• Combine images using multiple layers.

• Resize and reposition selections.

• Create a gradient clipping path.

• Remove the halo that may occur when copying and pasting selections of images.

Before you begin, make sure that you have correctly copied the Lessons folder from the CD in the back of this book onto your computer's hard disk. See "Copying the Classroom in a Book files" on page 3.

Getting started

For this lesson, you will be using the CIB Catalog you created at the start of the book. To open the CIB Catalog, follow these steps:

1   Start Photoshop Elements. In the Welcome Screen, click Organize in the row of shortcut buttons across the lower part of the Welcome Screen. If the CIB Catalog is open, skip to "Merging photos into a panorama" on the next page. If the CIB Catalog is not open, complete the following steps.

2   Choose File > Catalog.

3   In the Catalog Manager dialog box, select the CIB Catalog under Catalogs, and then click Open.

If you do not see the CIB Catalog file, review the procedures found in "Getting Started." See "Copying the Lessons files from the CD" on page 3, and "Creating a catalog" on page 4.

Merging photos into a panorama

The images you'll use for this first exercise are two slightly overlapping photos taken of Mont Saint Michel in France. The camera lens used for these shots did not have a wide enough angle to capture the entire scene. These pictures provide an ideal opportunity for learning how to create panoramas, having Photoshop Elements do most of the work for you.

1   If the Organizer is not currently active, switch to it now.

2   In the Keyword Tags palette, click the Find box next to the Lesson 10 keyword tag.

3   Ctrl-click to select the two pictures of Mont Saint Michel, named 10_01_a.jpg and 10_02_b.jpg.

Note: *If you don't see the file names in the Photo Browser, choose View > Show File Names.*

4   Choose File > New > Photomerge Panorama.

Photoshop Elements will load the Editor workspace in Full Edit mode and open the Photomerge dialog box.

5   Under Source Files in the Photomerge dialog box, select Files from the Use menu, and then click the Add Open Files button.

Note: *You can select more than two files to create a Photomerge Panorama composition.*

> *Select Folder from the Use menu, and then click Browse to add all photos from a specific folder on your hard disk. To remove photos from the selection, click to select them in the source file list, and then click Remove.*

6 Under Layout, select Auto, and then click OK.

Choosing a Photomerge layout option

Auto Photoshop analyzes the source images and applies either a Perspective or Cylindrical layout, depending on which produces a better photomerge.

Perspective Creates a consistent composition by designating one of the source images (by default, the middle image) as the reference image. The other images are then transformed (repositioned, stretched or skewed as necessary) so that overlapping content across layers is matched.

Cylindrical Reduces the "bow-tie" distortion that can occur with the Perspective layout by displaying individual images as on an unfolded cylinder. Overlapping content across layers is still matched. The reference image is placed at the center. Best suited for creating wide panoramas.

Reposition Only Aligns the layers and matches overlapping content, but does not transform (stretch or skew) any of the source layers.

Interactive Layout Choose this option to open the source images in a dialog and position them manually for the best result. See Create a photomerge interactively.

—From Photoshop Elements Help

7 Wait while Photoshop Elements creates the panorama and opens it in a new window.

That's it! You're basically done creating your panorama. All that remains to do is to crop the image and save your work. You'll do this in a moment. But first, let's have a closer look at how well Photoshop Elements did in merging the two images. (Depending on your source files, you may sometimes spot little problem areas and would then need to try a different layout option to merge you photos.)

8 In the Layers panel, click the eye icon (👁) for the top layer to hide it.

In the edit window, you can now see which part of the image in the second layer was used to create the panorama. The unused part is hidden by a layer mask. You can see a thumbnail of the layer mask in the Layers palette (with white representing the visible area and black the masked area).

9 Choose View > Actual Pixels. Then, use the Hand tool to drag the pictures so you can focus on the edge of the layer mask in the edit window. Repeatedly click the eye icon for the top layer to show either the complete panorama or just the part from the image in the second layer. When the complete panorama is shown, try to find any irregularities apparent along the edge of the layer mask (which you can only see when the top layer is hidden). Such irregularities could occur where some pixels along the edge of one layer mask appear misaligned with pixels along the edge of the adjoining layer mask. Use the Hand tool to drag to another area of the image along the edge of the layer mask and repeat your inspection.

Hide the top layer to reveal the edge of the image mask.

Show the top layer and check for irregularities along the edge of the image mask (now invisible).

10 If your inspection does not reveal any problem areas, make the top layer visible and you're ready to crop the picture and save it, as shown next. Should you find problems in your merged panorama, close the file without saving it, and then repeat the procedure trying a different Photomerge layout option in step 6. Using the interactive layout option, which gives you the most control when creating a panorama, is explained later in this lesson under "Creating a Photomerge Panorama interactively."

Cropping images

The Crop tool removes part of an image outside a selected area. Cropping is useful when you want to focus on a certain area of your photo. When you crop a photo, the resolution remains the same as in the original photo.

Since the photos that you just merged now have an irregular outline, you'll use the Crop tool to create a uniform edge.

1   Choose View > Fit on Screen.

2   Choose Image > Crop. A selection rectangle appears in the middle of your image, which you will adjust in step 3. You can also select the crop tool (⊞) from the toolbox and drag a cropping selection inside the image.

Note: You can crop images in Quick Fix mode the same way as in Full Edit mode. In Guided Edit mode you'll find a Crop Photo entry under Basic Photo Edits. If you are working in the Organizer, you can use the Crop tool in the Fix panel.

3   Drag the handles of the selection rectangle to make it as large as possible, being careful not to include any of the checkerboard areas where the image is transparent. Then, click the Commit button in the lower right corner of the selection rectangle.

4   Choose File > Save and save the merged image in the My CIB Work folder as **10_01_Work**, leaving Photoshop (*.PSD,*PDD) selected as the Format. Saving your file in Photoshop format enables you to later adjust individual layers, if necessary. When you convert to JPEG format, the layer information will be lost. You can export a JPEG version from the Photoshop file, for example, by using the Save for Web command.

Though it's not required for this image, when cropping you can specify any of the following settings in the options bar:

- The Aspect Ratio setting enables you to specify a preset crop. No Restriction lets you resize the image to any dimension. Use Photo Ratio retains the aspect ratio of the photo when you crop.

- The sizes listed specify preset sizes for the cropped photo. If you want your final output to be a specific size, such as 4 x 6 to fit a picture frame, choose that preset size.

- The Width and Height fields enable you to specify the physical dimensions of the image.

5 Choose File > Close to close the file 10_01_Work.psd, keeping the files 10_01_a.jpg and 10_02_b.jpg open in the Editor.

Creating a Photomerge Panorama interactively

If you need to manually rearrange your source images to create a panorama, select the interactive layout option in the Photomerge dialog box.

1 With the files 10_01_a.jpg and 10_02_b.jpg still open in the Editor, choose File > New > Photomerge Panorama.

2 Under Source Files in the Photomerge dialog box, select Files from the Use menu, and then click the Add Open Files button. Under Layout, select Interactive Layout, and then click OK.

3 Wait while Photoshop Elements opens the interactive Photomerge dialog box.

Note: *If the composition can't be automatically assembled, a message appears on-screen. You can assemble the composition manually in the Photomerge dialog box by dragging photos from the photo bin into the work area, and arranging the images where you want.*

4   You can fine-tune the panorama in the large Photomerge dialog box by doing the following:

• Under Navigator, use the controls to zoom in or out of the image. When zoomed in, drag the red view box to navigate within the image.

• Use the Select Image tool (✺) and click to select any of the photos in the large work area. Drag with the pointer or use the arrow keys on the keyboard to reposition.

• To remove a photo from the composition, drag it from the large work area onto the light box above. To add it again, drag it from the light box onto the work area.

• Select the Rotate Image tool (✺) and drag to rotate the selected photo.

• Choose between Reposition Only and Perspective under Settings.

• With Perspective selected under Settings, select the Set Vanishing Point tool (✺) and click in the image to set a new vanishing point.

5   When you're satisfied with your result, click OK to close the Photomerge dialog box.

The Photomerge dialog box closes, and Photoshop Elements goes to work. You'll see windows open and close as you wait for Photoshop Elements to create the panorama.

6   If you like your new composition better than the one you created in the previous exercise, crop the image and save your work in the My CIB Work folder.

7   Choose File > Close All to close all open windows. When asked whether you want to save your changes, click No.

8   Switch back to the Organizer.

Vanishing Point

A vanishing point is the point at which receding parallel lines seem to meet when seen in perspective. For example, as a road stretches out in front of you, it will seem to grow thinner the farther away it is, until it is almost nonexistent on the horizon. This is the vanishing point.

You can change the perspective of the Photomerge Panorama composition by specifying the location of the vanishing point. Select Perspective under Setting in the Photomerge dialog box, and then select the Vanishing Point tool and click in the image to reset the vanishing point location.

Panorama perspective with approximate location of the vanishing point, using the street curb as guidelines.

Creating group composites

Making the perfect group shot is a difficult task, especially if you have a large family with squirmy kids. For this purpose, Photoshop Elements offers a powerful photo-blending tool, called Photomerge Group Shot. Going through the following exercise will show you how multiple photos can be blended together to create one image with amazing perfection. Gone are the family photos where the eyes of one person are closed or another one has an odder than usual facial expression—with this new tool you can pick and choose the best parts of several pictures taken successively, and merge them together to form one perfect picture.

1   If the Organizer is not currently active, switch to it now.

2   In the Keyword Tags palette, click the Find box next to the Lesson 10 keyword tag.

3   Ctrl-click to select the three pictures named 10_02_a.psd, 10_02_b.psd, and 10_02_c.psd.

Note: Although this exercise uses three quite obviously different source images for demonstrational purpose, you would normally use the Photomerge Group Shot command to create a merged image from several very similar source images.

4 Choose File > New > Photomerge Group Shot.

The Photomerge Faces tool is similar to the Photomerge Group Shot tool, only specialized for work with individual faces. You can have a lot of fun merging different faces to one, e.g. merge parts of a picture of your face with the one of your spouse to predict the possible appearance of future offspring. In Guided Edit, select Faces under Photomerge to create your favorite Frankenface.

Photoshop Elements will load the Editor workspace in Guided Edit mode and start the Photomerge Group Shot task.

5 (Optional) If you want to work with photos not currently in the Organizer (or you want to avoid switching to the Organizer first), you can also open the photos directly in the Editor. Then, select the image thumbnails in the Project Bin, switch to Guided Edit mode, and select Group Shot under Photomerge.

6 From the Project Bin, drag the green framed image (10_02_c.psd) and drop it onto the Final image area on the right. Double-click the yellow framed image (10_02_b.psd) in the Project Bin to open it in the Source image area on the left.

7 Select the Zoom tool (🔍), and then zoom in on the image so you can see all of the girl in the Source image area and at least part of the girl in the Final image area. Use the Hand tool (✋) to reposition the image if necessary.

8 In the Guided Edit panel, select the Pencil Tool.

9 With the Pencil tool selected, draw one stroke from head to toe of the girl in the source image, as shown in the illustration on the next page. When you release the pointer, Photoshop will merge the entire girl from the source image (including her shadow on the stone!) into the final image. Seeing this tool's magic in action should give you some healthy mistrust whenever you come across an unbelievable photo in the future. If necessary, use the Pencil tool to add additional image areas from the source. Or, use the Eraser tool (🖌) to delete a stroke—or parts thereof—drawn accidentally with the Pencil tool. The image area copied to the final image will adjust accordingly.

Note: Sometimes it can be tricky to make the perfect selection. If you end up switching several times between Pencil tool and Eraser tool but can't get the selection right, using the Undo button (↩) and starting again from scratch is probably the best choice.

10 Double-click the blue framed image (10_02_a.psd) in the Project Bin to open it in the Source image area. Reposition the image in the source image area with the Hand tool, and then use the Pencil tool to add a third girl to the final image.

11   To see which parts of the three source images were used for the composition, click the Fit Screen button above the edit pane to see the entire image, and then select Show Regions in the Guided Edit panel.

12   Click the Actual Pixels button above the edit pane, and then use the Hand tool to position the image at a region boundary in the final image. Turn Show Regions off and on to look for imperfections along the region boundaries in the merged image. If necessary, use the Pencil or Eraser tool to add or remove areas from the respective source images in the final image. When you are satisfied with the result, click Done.

13   If necessary, use the Crop Photo tool (under Basic Photo Edits in the Guided Edit pane) to crop away distorted areas at the edges of the image. Select Use Photo Ratio from the Crop Box Size menu to keep the aspect ratio of the original photo. Then, click Done.

14 Choose File > Save and save the merged image in the My CIB Work folder as **10_02_Work**, leaving Photoshop (*.PSD,*PDD) selected as the Format. Switch to the Full Edit mode, choose File > Close All, and return to the Organizer.

Note: The File > Close All command is only available in the Full Edit mode. In Quick Fix and Guided Edit mode you can only close one file at a time using the File > Close command.

Combining multiple photographs in one file

In this project, you'll combine three photos in one. For the first image, you'll apply a clipping path to blend it into the background image. Then, you'll add a selection from the second image and learn about removing the fringe that may be visible in the combined image. Your final work file will contain all the original pixel information, so that you can go back and make adjustments whenever needed.

Arranging the image layers

In this first part of the project, you're going to combine two images. You'll make the photo of an airplane gradually fade into the sky of the background image.

As background image you'll use a picture of King Ludwig's castle in Bavaria, the masterpiece that inspired the design of Disney's Sleeping Beauty castle.

1   In the Keyword Tags palette of the Organizer, click the Find box next to the Lesson 10 keyword tag.

2   Ctrl-click to select the two pictures named 10_03_a.jpg and 10_03_b.jpg.

3   With both images selected in the Photo Browser, click the Editor button located near the top right corner of the Organizer window, and then choose Full Edit from the menu that appears.

4   In the Editor, choose Window > Images > Tile to view both images at the same time.

5   Click the title bar of the 10_03_b.jpg document window to make it the active window. Select the Move tool (⊹). While holding down the Shift key, click and drag the airplane image (10_03_b.jpg) into the castle picture (10_03_a.jpg). Release the pointer when you see a selection outline around the castle picture, and then release the Shift key.

6   Close the 10_03_b.jpg image window (the one you copied from).

7 In the Layers palette, select Layer 1 (airplane). Then, choose Image > Resize > Scale.

8 In the tool options bar, make sure Constrain Proportions is selected, and then type **50%** in the W (width) field. This scales the height and width by the same percentage.

9 Click the Commit button (✔) near the lower right corner of the selection rectangle to accept the changes.

10 With the Move tool still selected, click and drag the airplane on Layer 1 to the upper right corner of the background image. Then, click and drag the lower left handle of the selection rectangle to further reduce the size of the airplane image, as shown in the illustration below.

11 Release the pointer, and then click the Commit button (✔) to accept the changes.

Creating a gradient clipping path

A clipping path serves as a kind of template that allows part of an image to show while hiding the rest by making it transparent.

In the next steps you'll create a gradient that changes from fully opaque to fully transparent, and then use this gradient as a clipping path to blend the castle and aircraft layers together.

1 In the Layers palette, click the New Layer button () to create and select a new, blank layer, named Layer 2.

2 In the toolbox, select the Gradient tool (■), and then select the Default Foreground and Background Colors icon, or press the D key on your keyboard.

3 In the tool options bar, click the arrow to open the gradient selection menu. Locate the Foreground to Transparent thumbnail. Its name appears in a tooltip when you roll the cursor over it.

4 Double-click the Foreground to Transparent thumbnail to select that gradient and to close the gradient selection menu.

5 Make sure that the other settings in the tool options bar are as follows:

- Radial Gradient (■)

- Mode: Normal

- Opacity: 100%

- Reverse is deselected

- Transparency is selected

6 With the Gradient tool selected, click in the center of the airplane in Layer 1 and draw a short line downwards. Then, release the pointer.

When you release the pointer, you'll see a black spot that is opaque where it covers the airplane, gradually becoming transparent towards the edges of the image. Next, you will use this gradient as clipping path for the image of the airplane in Layer 1, making the airplane visible while its surrounding sky gradually fades into the sky of the background castle image.

Applying the clipping path to a layer

With your gradient layer completed, it's time to put it to work.

1 In the Layers palette, drag the new gradient layer, Layer 2, under Layer 1.

2 Select Layer 1, now the top layer, and then choose Layer > Group with Previous.

This action defines Layer 2 as the clipping path for Layer 1. In the Layers palette, Layer 1 is indented and shows an arrow pointing down to Layer 2. In the document window, the airplane image now blends nicely with the castle picture.

3 Choose File > Save As.

4 In the Save As dialog box, name the file **10_03_Work** and save it in the My CIB Work folder, with Photoshop (PSD) as Format and the Layers option selected. If Save in Version Set with Original is selected, deselect it before you click Save. If the Photoshop Elements Format Options dialog box appears, keep Maximize Compatibility selected and click OK.

Creating a clean edge with defringing

Defringing is used to remove those annoying bits of color that come along when copying and pasting a part of an image or deleting a selected background. When the copied area is pasted onto another background color, or the selected background is deleted, you can often see a fine halo around your selection. Defringe blends the halo away so you won't see a hard line.

Now you'll composite an image of a family so that they appear to be standing in front of the fence in the castle picture by selecting and deleting the background and using the defringe feature.

1   Switch to the Organizer, select the file 10_03_c.jpg, the picture of the family, and then open it in Full Edit mode.

2   With the family image (10_03_c.jpg) as the active window in the Editor, choose Select > All, then Edit > Copy, and then File > Close. Select the Background layer of the 10_03_Work.psd image, and then choose Edit > Paste. The image of the family is placed on a new layer, named Layer 3, just above the background layer.

3   With Layer 3, the family image, still selected in the Layers palette, choose Image > Resize > Scale.

4   In the tool options bar, make sure Constrain Proportions is selected, and then type **80%** in the W (width) field.

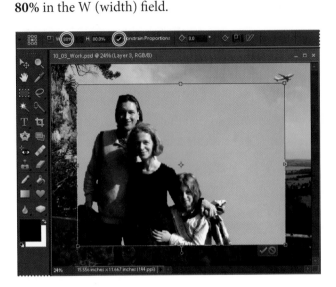

5   Click the Commit button (✔) near the lower right corner of the selection rectangle to accept the changes.

6   If necessary, scroll to see the lower left corner of the image in the document window. Select the Move tool. Click and drag the image in Layer 3, the family, to position it in the lower left corner of the castle image.

7   In the toolbox, select the Magic Wand tool (✦). In the tool options bar, enter **25** as Tolerance, select Anti-alias, and deselect Contiguous as well as All Layers. Then, click on the pink-colored background of the family picture. If necessary, hold down the Shift key and click to select any remaining unselected pink areas of the background.

8   Then, press the Delete key to delete the pink-colored background. Press Ctrl+D, or choose Select > Deselect to clear the selection.

9   Select the Zoom tool and zoom in on the lower left corner of the image to the area between the man's right hand and his sweater. The halo around that area, or fringe, is clearly visible.

10   Choose Enhance > Adjust Color > Defringe Layer. In the Defringe dialog box, enter **1** pixel for the width and click OK.

Notice how the fringe is eliminated.

Before applying the Defringe Layer command   *After applying the Defringe Layer command*

11   Double-click the Hand tool in the toolbox, or click the Fit Screen button in the tool options bar, to fit the image in the window and see your completed work.

12   (Optional) With the Layer 3 still selected in the Layers palette, select the Move tool in the toolbox. Then, drag the top right handle of the selection rectangle to enlarge the image of the family to become more the focus of the composition.

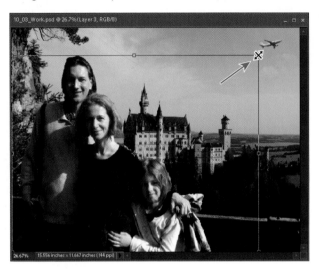

13   Click the Commit button (✔) near the lower right corner of the selection rectangle to accept the changes.

14   Choose File > Save to save your changes to the file. Then close the document and return to the Organizer.

Congratulations, you've completed the last exercise in this lesson. You've learned how to create a composite image by arranging layers and using a gradient layer as a clipping path. You also used the Defringe option, which eliminates the halo of edge pixels that remain from a deleted background.

Review

▶ **Review questions**

1   In the Photomerge dialog box, which tools can be used to fine-tune a panorama created from multiple images, and how do they work?

2   What does the Photomerge Group Shot tool do?

3   Why is it when you think you're finished with a transformation you cannot select another tool or perform other actions?

4   What is a fringe and how can you remove it?

▶ **Review answers**

1   The Select Image tool is used to select a specific image from within the merged panorama. This tool can also be used to drag an image so that it lines up more closely with the other images in the panorama. The Rotate Image tool is used to rotate merged images so that their content aligns seamlessly.

2   With the Photomerge Group Shot tool you can pick and choose the best parts of several pictures taken successively, and merge them together to form one perfect picture.

3   Photoshop Elements is waiting for you to confirm the transformation by clicking the Commit button, or by double-clicking inside the transformation boundary.

4   A fringe is that annoying bit of color that comes along when copying and pasting a part of an image or deleting a selected background. When the copied area is pasted onto another background color, or the selected background is deleted, you can see a fine halo around your selection. The Defringe Layer command (Enhance > Adjust Color > Defringe Layer) blends the halo away so you won't see a hard line.

11 | Advanced Editing Techniques

In this lesson, you will discover advanced editing techniques in Adobe Photoshop Elements. Using innovative tools that enable you to improve the quality and clarity of your images, you will learn to do the following:

- Use camera raw images from your digital camera.
- Save conversions in the DNG format.
- Use histograms to understand the characteristics of an image.
- Improving the quality of highlights and shadows.
- Resize and sharpen an image.
- Create effects with the filter gallery.
- Use the Cookie Cutter tool.

This lesson assumes that you are already familiar with the overall features of the Photoshop Elements work area, and recognize the two ways in which you can use Photoshop Elements: the Editor and the Organizer. If you need to learn more about these items, see Photoshop Elements Help and the Adobe Photoshop Elements Getting Started Guide. This lesson also builds on the skills and concepts covered in the earlier lessons.

Before you begin, make sure that you have correctly copied the Lessons folder from the CD in the back of this book onto your computer's hard disk. See "Copying the Classroom in a Book files" on page 3.

In this lesson, you will use the CIB Catalog you created earlier in the book. If necessary, open this catalog by choosing File > Catalog in Organizer mode, and then click Open.

What is a raw image?

Raw files are referred to as such because they are unprocessed by the digital camera or image scanner, unlike many of the other image file formats that you may recognize, such as JPEG or GIF.

Whether you are a professional or amateur photographer, it can be difficult to understand all the process settings on your digital camera. Processing images may degrade the quality of an image. One solution is to use the camera's raw setting. Raw images are derived directly from the camera's sensors, prior to any camera processing. Not all digital cameras offer the ability to shoot raw images, but many of the newer and more advanced cameras have this option.

Note: Depending upon the camera used to take the picture, raw file names have different extensions. Examples are Canon's .CRW and .CR2, Epson's .ERF, Fuji's .RAF, Kodak's .KDE and .DER, Minolta's .MRW, Olympus'.ORF, Pentax's .PTX and .PEF, Panasonic's .RAW, and the various flavors of Nikon's .NEF.

You can open a raw file in Photoshop Elements, process it, and save it—instead of relying on the camera to process the file. Working with camera raw files lets you adjust proper white balance, tonal range, contrast, color saturation, and sharpening, even after the image has been taken.

The benefits of a raw image

Raw images are high-quality image files that contain the maximum amount of original image data in a relatively small file size. Though larger than a compressed file, such as JPEG, raw images contain more data and use less space than a TIFF image.

Flexibility is another benefit, since many of the camera settings like sharpening, white balance, levels, and color adjustments can be undone when using Photoshop Elements. For instance, adjustments to exposure can be undone and recalculated based on the raw data. Also, because raw has 12 bits of available data, you are able to extract shadow and highlight detail that would have been lost in the 8 bits/channel JPEG or TIFF format.

Raw files provide an archival image format, much like a digital negative, but one that outlasts the usefulness and longevity of film. You can reprocess the file repeatedly to achieve the results you want. Photoshop Elements doesn't save your changes to the original raw file; rather, it saves the last setting you used to process it.

Workflow overview

To use raw files, you need to set your camera to save files in its own raw file format. Photoshop Elements can open raw files only from supported cameras. For an up-to-date list of supported cameras, please visit: http://www.adobe.com/products/photoshop/cameraraw.html.

After processing the raw image file with the Camera Raw window, you open the image in Photoshop Elements, where you can work with it in the same way as any other photo. Then, you can save the file in any format supported by Photoshop Elements, such as PSD.

Note: The RAW plug-in, which is used to open files from a digital camera, is updated over time as new cameras are supported. It may be necessary to replace your plug-in with the latest version from the www.adobe.com Web site.

Getting started

Before you start working, take a few moments to make sure that your work area is set up for these projects.

1   Start Adobe Photoshop Elements, and choose Edit in the Welcome screen.

2   Select the Full Edit mode.

3   Choose File > Open. Navigate to the Lesson11 folder and open the file 11_01.ORF, a raw image of a coastline generated from an Olympus digital camera.

4   Make sure that Preview is selected in the Camera Raw dialog box that comes up. *(See illustration on the next page.)*

The camera raw window provides the tools that you need to make adjustments to your image.
A. *Zoom tool.* *B*. *Hand tool.* *C*. *White Balance tool.* *D*. *Crop tool.* *E*. *Straighten tool.* *F*. *Red Eye Removal.*
G. *Open Preferences dialog.* *H*. *Rotate counter-clockwise.* *I*. *Rotate clockwise.* *J*. *Histogram.* *K*. *White Balance*
L. *Zoom level.* *M*. *Bit Depth.*

When you open a camera raw file, Photoshop Elements reads information in the file to
see which model of camera created it, and then applies the appropriate camera settings
to the image. You can save the current settings as the default for the camera that created
the image, by clicking the palette menu—located in the top right corner of the palette—
and selecting Save New Camera Raw Defaults. There you can also use the Photoshop
Elements default settings for your camera by selecting Reset Camera Raw Defaults.

White balance controls for camera raw

A digital camera records the white balance at the time of exposure as metadata, which you can see when you open the file in the Camera Raw dialog box. This setting usually yields the correct color temperature. You can adjust it if the white balance is not quite right. The Adjust tab in the Photoshop Camera Raw dialog box includes the following three controls for correcting a color cast in your image:

White Balance

Sets the color balance of the image to reflect the lighting conditions under which the photo was taken. In some cases, choosing a white balance from the White Balance menu provides satisfactory results. In many cases, you may want to customize the white balance using the Temperature and Tint adjustments.

Temperature

Fine-tunes the white balance to a custom color temperature. Set the color temperature using the Kelvin color temperature scale. Move the slider to the left to correct a photo taken with light of a lower color temperature; the plug-in makes the image colors bluer to compensate for the lower color temperature (yellowish) of the ambient light. Conversely, move the slider to the right to correct a photo taken with a light of higher color temperature; the plug-in makes the image colors warmer (yellowish) to compensate for the higher color temperature (bluish) of the ambient light.

Tint

Fine-tunes the white balance to compensate for a green or magenta tint. Move the slider to the left (negative values) to add green to the photo; move it to the right (positive values) to add magenta.

To adjust the white balance quickly, select the White Balance tool, and then click an area in the preview image that should be a neutral gray or white. The Temperature and Tint sliders automatically adjust to make the selected color exactly neutral (if possible). If you're clicking whites, choose a highlight area that contains significant white detail rather than a specular highlight.

—From Photoshop Elements Help

Improving a camera raw image

There are two palettes in the Camera Raw window: Basic and Detail. The Basic palette gives you the controls to fine-tune options not available within the standard edit tools in Photoshop Elements. The Detail palette gives you controls to adjust sharpening and noise. You will use the controls on the Basic palette.

Note: Any correction you make to an image removes data from that image. Because you are working with much more information in a RAW file, any changes you make to the settings, such as exposure and white balance, will have less impact on the image than if you made drastic changes in a .PSD, TIFF, or JPEG file.

Adjusting the white balance

Presets are helpful if you need to accommodate for color casts introduced by poor lighting conditions when the image was taken. For example, if your camera was not set up correctly to deal with a sunny day, you can fix resulting problems in the image here by selecting Daylight from the White Balance menu.

1 In the White Balance menu, experiment by trying some of the presets available in the White Balance menu. Notice the change in the preview window as you select various White Balance presets. In the next section, you will discover why selecting the correct white balance is very important to the overall look of the image.

2 Select Cloudy as setting.

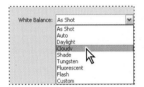

3 Before moving to the next part of this lesson where you'll use another way to improve the color balance, select As Shot from the White Balance menu.

By understanding what a neutral color is and how it works, you can easily remove color tints from an image in the Raw window. For this you need to locate a neutral color with the White Balance tool. Neutral colors include black, white, and gray.

4 Let's first zoom into the image by selecting the zoom level of 100% in the lower left corner of your Camera Raw dialog box.

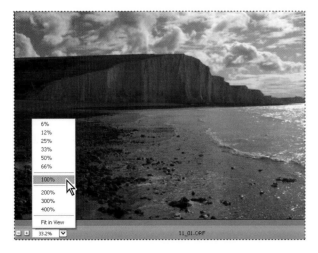

5   Select the Hand tool (✋) from the tools at the top of the Camera Raw dialog box, and move into the center of the image where you see parts of the blue sky as well as the green of the grass.

6   Select the White Balance tool (✐) right next to the Hand tool.

7   Locate a neutral color in the image—a good example is a white or gray cloud—then use the White balance tool to click on it.

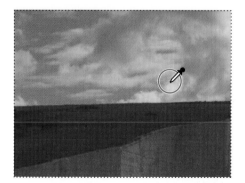

The White Balance is now at Custom, and the image is better balanced.

Working with tint control

Using the White Balance tool accurately removes any color cast, or tint, from an image. Depending upon the subject matter, you might want a slight, controlled color tint. In this instance, while the color temperature seems fine, you will fine-tune the green/magenta balance of the image using the Tint controls.

1   Zoom out to view the entire picture by either clicking the Zoom tool or by selecting the zoom level of 33% (depending of the size of your computer screen) in the lower left corner of your Camera Raw dialog box.

2   Check out the Temperature slider in the Basic palette by dragging it to the left and to the right. You'll see how the colors of the image turn cooler (more blue), or warmer (more orange). While the original temperature of the image seems fine in this case, this slider could help you on other occasions, for toning down the warm glow in tungsten lighting, for example.

3   Go back to the original color temperature setting of 5350 by either dragging the slider or typing **5350** into the white box next to the Temperature slider.

4   Click the Tint slider. Either click and drag the slider slightly to the right, or type **+20** into the box.

Using the tone controls on a raw image

The Tonal controls are located under the White Balance controls in the raw window. In this next section, you'll find out how to use these controls to adjust for incorrect exposure, as well as check shadows, adjust brightness, contrast, and saturation.

Before you make adjustments, it is important that you understand these essential items:

Exposure is a measure of the amount of light in which a photo was taken. Underexposed digital photos are too dark; overexposed ones, too light. Use this control to recover the lighter, or blown-out information from overexposed images.

Recovery attempts to recover details from highlights. Camera Raw can reconstruct some details from areas in which one or two color channels are clipped to white or black. Clipping occurs when a pixel's color values are higher than the highest value or lower than the lowest value that can be represented in the image; overbright values are clipped to output white, and overdark values are clipped to output black.

Fill Light recovers details from shadows, without brightening blacks. Using Fill Light is similar to using the shadows portion of the Photoshop Shadow/Highlight filter.

Blacks specifies which input levels are mapped to black in the final image. Increasing Blacks expands the areas that are mapped to black. This sometimes creates the appearance of increased contrast in the image.

Brightness adjusts the brightness of the image, much as the Exposure slider does. However, instead of clipping the image in the highlights (areas that are completely white, no detail) or shadows (areas that are completely black, no detail), Brightness compresses the highlights and expands the shadows when you move the slider to the right. In general, use the Brightness slider to adjust the overall brightness after you set the white and black clipping points with the Exposure and Shadow sliders.

Contrast is the difference in brightness between light and dark areas of an image. Contrast determines the number of shades in the image. An image without contrast can appear "washed out." Use the Contrast slider to adjust the contrast of the midtones after setting the Exposure, Shadow, and Brightness values.

Clarity sharpens the definition of edges in the image. This process helps restore detail and sharpness that tonal adjustments may reduce.

Saturation is the purity, or strength, of a color. Also called chroma. A fully saturated color contains no gray. Saturation controls make colors more vivid (less black or white added) or more muted (more black or white added).

Vibrance adjusts the saturation so that clipping is minimized as colors approach full saturation, acting on all lower saturated colors but having less impact on higher saturated colors. Vibrance also prevents skin tones from becoming oversaturated.

You will check the Exposure of this image, and make adjustments based upon the lightness values in this image.

1   Hold down the Alt key while moving the Exposure slider. This shows the clipping (what parts of the image will be forced towards white) as you adjust the exposure. We moved the slider to +0.25.

Hold down the Alt key while sliding the Exposure to see highlight clipping.

Now you will adjust the shadow.

2   Click and drag the Recovery slider to 60.

3 Hold down the Alt key and click and drag the Black slider. Any areas that appear in the clipping preview will be forced to a solid black. Release when only the deep areas of shadow in the image appear as black. We moved the slider to 10.

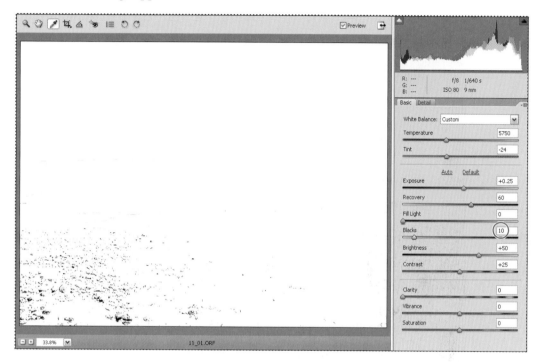

4 Select the Brightness slider and press the up arrow on the keyboard to increase the value to 64.

5 Select the Contrast slider and press the up arrow key on the keyboard to increase the value to +50.

6 Drag the Clarity slider to 28.

💡 *For an interesting effect, you can drag the Saturation slider all the way to the left to neutralize your image, essentially creating a three-color grayscale.*

The image, which was shot at a cloudy day and looked a little dull, now shows a larger range of detail and is more vivid in colors. *(See illustration on the next page.)*

Saving the image

You can reprocess this raw file repeatedly to achieve the results you want by saving in the DNG format. Photoshop Elements doesn't save your changes to the original raw file, but it saves the last settings you used to process it.

About the DNG format

Raw file formats are becoming common in digital photography. However, each camera manufacturer has its own proprietary raw format. This means that not every raw file can be read by software other than that provided with the camera. This may make it difficult to use these images in the future, as the camera manufacturers might not support these file formats indefinitely. Proprietary formats are also a problem if you want to use software other than that supplied by the camera manufacturers.

To help alleviate these problems, you can save raw images from Photoshop Elements in the DNG format, a publicly available archival format for raw files generated by digital cameras. The DNG format provides an open standard for files created by different camera models, and helps to ensure that you will be able to access your files in the future.

1   To convert and save the image, click Save Image In the 11_01.ORF raw dialog box. The Save Options dialog box appears.

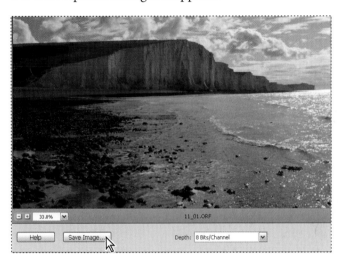

2   Click the Select Folder button under Destination. In the Select Destination Folder dialog box, select your My CIB Work folder, and then click Select to return to the Save Options dialog box.

3   Under File Naming, leave Document Name selected in the menu on the left. Click the menu on the right and select 1 Digit Serial Number. This adds the number 1 following the name.

4 Click Save. The file, along with the present settings, will be saved in DNG format, which you can reprocess repeatedly.

5 Click Open Image in the right lower corner of the camera raw dialog box. Your image will open in the Editor window of Photoshop Elements Editor.

6 Choose File > Save. Navigate to the My CIB Work folder. Name the file **11_011_Work.psd**. Make sure the selection in the Format menu is Photoshop, and then click Save.

7 Choose File > Close.

You've now experienced some of the pros of using camera raw formats. However, even though this format gives you more control and lets you edit your image in a non-destructive way, a lot of professionals choose not to use raw format. Raw files are usually considerably bigger than high-quality JPEGs and take much longer to be saved in your camera—quite a disadvantage for action shots or when you're taking a lot of pictures.

About histograms

Many of your images may be saved using a variety of formats, including JPEG, TIFF, or PSD. For these images, you will make your adjustments in the Full Editor. In this part of the lesson, you will discover how to use the histogram to understand what changes can be made to your images to improve their quality.

In this section, you will open an image that was shot with poor lighting and also has a slight magenta cast to it. Many digital cameras introduce a slight cast into images.

Using histograms

A histogram is a chart displaying the tonal ranges present in an image. The Histogram palette, located under Window > Histogram, shows whether the image contains enough detail in the shadows, midtones, and highlights. A histogram also helps you recognize where changes need to be made in the image.

Tonal corrections, such as lightening an image, remove information from the image. Excessive correction causes posterization, or banding in the image.

Histograms show detail and tonal range of an image.
A. Shadows. B. Midtones. C. Highlights.

In this histogram low midtone levels are apparent.

This histogram reveals that the image is already lacking detail.
Further corrections will degrade the image even more.

Understanding highlights and shadows

In the next part of this lesson, you will open an image and adjust the highlight and shadow. You will also make additional tonal corrections while keeping an eye on the Histogram palette.

1   In the Editor choose File > Open, then choose the file 11_02.psd in your Lesson 11 folder. It's the image of the girls from the previous page.

2   Choose File > Save As and navigate to the My CIB Work folder. Save the image as **11_02_Work.psd**. Click Save.

3   Make sure the Full Edit button is selected.

4   If it is not already visible, choose Window > Histogram.

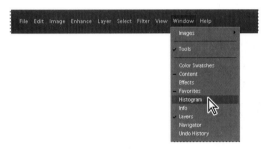

5   In order to see your adjustments more directly, you can drag the Histogram palette out of the Palette bin and place it next to the face of the girl. Notice that the face is a little dark.

*This image needs more information in the middle areas
and less information in the highlights and shadows.*

According to the Histogram, there is a lack of data in the middle (midtones) of the image. You will adjust the tonal range of this image using Levels.

Adjusting levels

1   Choose Enhance > Adjust Lighting > Levels. The Levels dialog box appears.

You will use the shadow, midtone, and highlight sliders, as well as the Set Black Point, Set Gray Point, and Set White Point eyedroppers in this exercise. Although the range of midtones is the most problematic area of this image, it is important to first adjust the highlights and shadows.

The Levels dialog box.
A. Shadow. **B**. Midtone. **C**. Highlight. **D**. Set Black Point.
E. Set Gray Point. **F**. Set White Point.

2   Double-click the Set White Point eyedropper.

This opens the Color Picker dialog box. In this dialog box, you will choose the highlight of your image. You will designate the lightest, non-specular point in the image as being the highlight.

Note: Specular highlights are the reflections of light on the surface of an object. The shiny spots on chrome or jewelry are typical examples. Pure white on an image is generally reserved for such specular highlights.

3   In the Color Picker dialog box, type **240** in the R (Red), G (Green), and B (Blue) text fields. This defines the light point of your image as a light gray, not pure white. Pure white is reserved for specular highlights in an image. Click OK in the Color Picker dialog box.

Double-click the Set White Point eyedropper to change the highlight value in the Color Picker.

4   Hold down the Alt key and click (don't drag!) the Highlight slider. The clipping preview for the highlight appears. The visible areas are the lightest areas of the image. Release the Alt key to see you've located the lightest portion of the sky in the image.

5   Select the Set White Point eyedropper and click the portion of your image that appeared in the clipping preview (the light part of the sky in the upper right corner). Notice how the image becomes slightly lighter, and small changes occur in the histogram.

You will now set the Shadow area, using a slightly different technique.

6   Hold down the Alt key and click then drag the shadow slider to the right until the area below the left ear and the darkest areas of the image appear as dark spots in the shadow clipping preview. Then release the pointer and the Alt key. We adjusted the shadow input value to 16. *(See illustration on next page.)*

7 Visually lighten the midtone by selecting the midtone slider (the gray triangle in the center) and dragging it to the left. We adjusted our midtone to 1.50.

8 Notice the change in the Histogram as you make this change. Compare the old data (displayed in gray) to the data showing the correction that you are now making (displayed in black). Some gaps will be created, but you want to avoid creating very large gaps. Even if the image still looks fine on screen, large gaps may cause a loss of data that is visible when printed.

💡 *If you have easily identified neutrals in your image, you can remove a color cast quickly using the Set Gray Point dropper. Neutrals are areas in the image that contain only a gray tone, or an area containing as few colors as possible.*

9 Click OK to close the Levels dialog box. When the Adobe Photoshop Elements alert dialog box appears, click Yes. You should save the new target colors so you do not have to set the white point every time you use the Levels dialog box to make adjustments.

10 Select Edit > Undo Levels, or press Ctrl+Z to see how the image looked prior to changing the highlights and shadows. Choose Edit > Redo Levels, or Press Ctrl+Y to bring back the correction you made.

Before and after adjusting the levels.

Leave this image open for the next part of this lesson.

About unsharp mask

In this exercise, you will add some crispness to the image, and make it look much better when printed. Using the sharpening tools correctly can significantly improve an image.

You'll use the Unsharp mask feature in Photoshop Elements. How can something be unsharp and yet sharpen an image? The term unsharp mask has it roots in the print production industry: the technique was implemented by making an out-of-focus negative film—the unsharp mask—and then printing the original in a sandwich with this unsharp mask. This produced a halo around the edges of objects—optically giving them more definition.

> 💡 *If you are planning to resize an image, resize first, and then apply the Unsharp mask filter.*

1   With the 11_02_Work.psd image still open, choose Image > Resize > Image Size. This image needs to be made smaller, but with a higher resolution (pixels per inch).

2   If necessary, deselect the Resample Image check box at the bottom of the dialog box, and then type **300** in the Resolution text field. Notice that the width and height increments adjust. This method increases the resolution in the image without losing information.

Resolution means the fineness of detail you can see in an image. Measured in pixels per inch (ppi): the more pixels per inch, the greater the resolution. Generally, the higher the resolution of your image, the better the printed image.

3   Now select Resample Image, to reduce the height and width of the image and not affect the resolution. Click OK.

Always resize before sharpening an image.

4   Choose File > Save. Keep the file open for the next part of this lesson.

Applying the Unsharp Mask filter

Before applying any filter in Adobe Photoshop Elements, it is best to be at 100% view.

1   With the 11_face_work.psd image still open, choose View > Actual pixels.

2   Choose Enhance > Unsharp Mask. The Unsharp Mask dialog box appears.

The amount of unsharp masking you apply is determined by the subject matter. A portrait, such as this image, should be softer than an image of an object such as an automobile. The adjustments range from 100 to 500, with 500 being the sharpest.

3   Slide the Amount adjustment or type **100** in the Adjustment text field. Leave the Radius at 1 pixel.

4   Increase the Threshold only slightly to 2 pixels. Threshold is a key control in this dialog box, as it tells the filter what not to sharpen, In this case the value 2 tells it to not sharpen a pixel if it is within 2 shades of the pixel next to it.

Disable the preview in the Unsharp Mask window by clicking and holding down on the preview pane. When you release the mouse, the preview is enabled again. To reveal other portions of the image, click and drag in the preview pane.

5   Click OK to close the Unsharp Mask dialog box.

Image with no sharpening.   Image with unsharp mask applied.

6   Choose File > Save, and then choose File > Close.

As you've seen, the Unsharp Mask filter does not mysteriously correct the focus of your image. It only gives the impression of crispness by increasing the contrast of the pixels. As a rule of thumb, the Unsharp Mask filter should be used only once as final step of your enhancements. When using it more often, you'll run into the risk of over sharpening your image and giving it a flaky, grainy look.

Note: There are additional ways to adjust the sharpness of your photos: Choose Enhance > Auto Sharpen, or for even control Enhance > Adjust Sharpness.

Creating effects using the filter gallery

You can experiment and apply interesting filter effects using the Filter Gallery, which enables you to apply multiple filters at the same time, as well as to re-arrange the order in which they affect the image. This gives you a lot of control over the way you want each filter to affect your image. Obviously, it's up to you to make the most out of these filters and to utilize them with intelligence. Have a look at "About Filters" in Photoshop Help to find out more about the different filters.

Not all filters are available from the Filter Gallery. Some are available only as individual commands from the Filter menu. Also, you cannot apply effects and layer styles from the Filter Gallery, as you can from the Effects palette.

1   Select the file named 11_03.psd in your Lesson 11 folder, and then choose Edit > Go to Full Edit from the shortcuts bar.

2   Choose File > Save As, and navigate to the My CIB Work folder. Name the file **11_03_Work**. With Photoshop (*.PSD,*.PDD) selected as Format, click Save.

Because many filters use the active foreground and background colors to create effects, take a moment and set them now.

3   Click the Default Foreground and Background Color swatches at the bottom of the toolbar. This resets the default black foreground and white background colors.

4   Choose Filter > Filter Gallery. The Filter Gallery dialog box appears.

5   If necessary, use the menu in the lower left corner of the dialog box to set the magnification level at 100%. This view brings the image much closer so that the effects of the filters you apply are more obvious.

6   In the preview pane, click and hold the pointer to temporarily change the cursor into the hand tool (🖐). While holding down the pointer, drag the image so that you can see the faces and hats of the two kids on the left in the preview pane.

Listed in the Filter Gallery are several categories of filters from which you can choose.

7   Expand the Brush Strokes category by clicking the arrow to the left of Brush Strokes.

8   Play around with the different sliders—the filter is applied in the preview image.

9   Click the New Effect layer (⬕) on the bottom right, and then select Film Grain from the Artistic filters. Both the Brush Strokes and Film Grain filters are applied simultaneously.

10   Using the Grain slider, change the value to 10, and then change the Highlight Area to 11 with the Highlight Area slider.

The Filter Gallery enables you to apply multiple filters simultaneously.

11   Click the New Effects layer again. If necessary, scroll down in the list of filters to be able to see the Stylize category. Expand the Stylize filters and select Glowing Edges. Again, your image has changed totally. *(See illustration on the next page.)*

💡 *It's a good idea to apply filters to a duplicate layer of your image, as it is not possible to undo filters after you've saved your file. Press Ctrl+J to duplicate a layer.*

Experimenting with filters in the gallery

The Possibilities are endless for the effects that you might create in your image by combining different filters at different settings.

1   Experiment with the three filters that you have applied, turning them off or on by clicking the eye icon (👁) to the left of the filters.

2   Re-arrange the filters, for example by clicking and dragging the Film Grain filter to the top of the list.

3 There is no need to apply the changes to the image. Click Cancel to close the Filter Gallery dialog box.

4 Keep the file open for the next part of the lesson.

Using the Cookie Cutter tool

The Cookie Cutter tool enables you to crop an image into a shape that you choose. Use the Cookie Cutter tool to clip a photo into a fun or interesting shape. In this part of the lesson, you'll add a heart shape to the image.

1 Select the Cookie Cutter tool from the toolbox.

2 Click the Shapes menu on the tool options bar to view a library of shapes from which you can choose. The visible selections are the default shapes.

There are many more cutout shapes available. Click the double-arrow in the upper right corner of the default shape selection to see a menu of 22 different categories from which you can choose.

3 Double-click to select the shape named Heart Card (the shape of a heart), which fits well to the image.

Note: The assigned name for each shape appears as a tooltip when you move the pointer over its thumbnail image.

4   Under Set Shape Options, select From Center.

Set Shape Options:

Unconstrained—Draws the shape to any size or dimension you'd like.

Defined Proportions—Keeps the height and width of the cropped shape in proportion.

Defined Size—Crops the photo to the exact size of the shape you choose.

Fixed Size—Specifies exact measurements for the finished shape.

From Center—Draws the shape from the center.

Enter a value for **Feather** to soften the edges of the finished shape.

Note: Feathering softens the edges of the cropped image so that the edges fade out and blend in with the background.

—From Adobe Photoshop Elements Help

5   Click and drag across the document window to create the shape on the image. While dragging, you can press the Shift key to keep the original aspect ratio of the shape, or press the Space key to reposition the shape. After releasing the pointer, you can use the handles on the selection rectangle to scale the object. Click inside the selection rectangle and drag to reposition it.

6   Click the Commit button (✔) near the lower right corner of the selection rectangle, or press Enter to finish cropping. If you want to cancel the cropping operation, click the Cancel button (◒), or press the Esc key.

7   Choose File > Save. Then, choose File > Close.

Congratulations, you have finished the lesson on advanced editing techniques in Adobe Photoshop Elements. You discovered how to take advantage of the raw features and adjust images using the histogram as a reference. You also found out how to create effects using the filter gallery and make cropping frames using the Cookie Cutter tool.

Learning more

We hope you've gained confidence, skill, and knowledge about using Photoshop Elements to bring out the best in your photographs. But this book is just the start. You can learn even more by studying the Photoshop Elements Help system, which is built into the application, by choosing Help > Photoshop Elements Help. Also, don't forget to look for tutorials, tips, and expert advice on the Adobe Web site, www.adobe.com.

Review

▶ Review questions

1   What is a camera raw image, and what are three benefits to using it?

2   What different methods can you use to control the white balance in the raw window?

3   What tools can you use in the Levels control to set highlight and shadow?

4   What is the Cookie Cutter tool used for?

▶ Review answers

1   A raw file is one that is unprocessed by a digital camera. Not all cameras create raw files.

Benefits include the following:

Flexibility—many of the camera settings, such as sharpening, white balance, levels and color adjustments can be undone when using Photoshop Elements.

Quality—because RAW has 12 bits of available data, you are able to extract shadow and highlight detail that would have been lost in an 8 bits/channel JPEG or TIFF format.

Archive—RAW files provide an archival image format, much like a digital negative, but one that outlasts the usefulness and longevity of film. You can reprocess the file repeatedly to achieve the results you want.

2   Three methods to control the White balance in the Raw window include:

•   Setting the white balance in an image automatically by using the White Balance eyedropper tool in the raw window. Selecting the White Balance eyedropper and clicking on a neutral automatically adjusts the Temperature and Tint sliders.

•   Selecting a preset white balance from the White Balance menu. Here you can choose from options that include corrections based upon variable such as whether the flash was used, it was a cloudy day, or the image was shot in fluorescent light, to name but a few.

•   Manually changing the Temperature and Tint adjustments by using the appropriate sliders under White Balance.

3 Use the Set Black Point and Set White Point eyedropper tools in the Levels dialog box.

- In the Levels dialog box you can double-click the Set Black Point and Set White Point tools to enter the desired values.

- To find the light point, you can Alt+drag the shadow or highlight sliders. This turns on the clipping preview.

- Select the darkest point with the Set Black Point tool by selecting the tool and clicking the darkest part of the image.

- Select the lightest point by using the Set White Point tool to click on the lightest part of the image.

4 The Cookie Cutter tool is used to clip an image in a variety of shapes. Use the default shapes in the Shape menu, or select from a variety of shape libraries available in the Shape dialog box palette.

Index

Production Notes

The *Adobe Photoshop Elements 6.0 Classroom in a Book* was created electronically using Adobe InDesign CS2. Additional art was produced using Adobe Illustrator CS2, Adobe Photoshop CS2, and Adobe Photoshop Elements 6.0.

Team credits

The following individuals contributed to the development of new and updated lessons for this edition of the *Adobe Photoshop Elements Classroom in a Book*:

Project coordinators, technical writers: Torsten Buck & Katrin Straub

Production: Manneken Pis Productions (www.manneken.com)

Copyediting & Proofreading: Ross Evans

Designer: Katrin Straub

Special thanks to Christine Yarrow.

Typefaces used

Set in the Adobe Minion Pro and Adobe Myriad Pro OpenType families of typefaces. More information about OpenType and Adobe fonts is available at Adobe.com.

Photo Credits

Photographic images and illustrations supplied by Katrin Straub, Torsten Buck, Marianne Barcellona, and Adobe Systems Incorporated. Photos are for use only with the lessons in the book.